HEALTH CARE IN CRISIS

Essays on Health Services Under Capitalism

Edited by

Marlene Dixon and
Thomas Bodenheimer M.D.

A SYNTHESIS PUBLICATION
San Francisco

The first three articles in this collection were originally published between 1976 and 1977 in *Synthesis* (now *Contemporary Marxism*). The final article is also being published in the *Journal of Sociology and Social Welfare*, Vol. 7, No. 3, May 1980.

Published by Synthesis Publications
131 Townsend Street
San Francisco, California 94107

ISBN 0-89935-004-6
Library of Congress No. 79-90213
Copyright (c) 1980 by
Synthesis Publications

CONTENTS

Introduction

The United States is the richest and most powerful nation in human history. Yet Americans suffer the cruelest and most barbaric health system of the entire developed world.

—In the United States, 24 million members of the working class have no health insurance whatsoever, and 65 million have such poor coverage that they risk bankruptcy whenever they fall seriously ill.[1] At the same time, private health insurance companies collect more than $6 billion a year over and above what they pay out in health benefits.[2]

—In the United States, physicians (with average incomes over $70,000 a year) refuse to see patients who cannot pay; yet the same physicians yearly perform 2 million lucrative operations that are entirely unnecessary on people who can pay.[3]

—In the United States, the pharmaceutical industry profits to the tune of $1 billion per year while drug reactions, many from drugs that are entirely unnecessary, cause illness that costs over $1 billion per year and kill 130,000 people each year.[4]

—Hospitals may deny beds to patients who cannot pay $300 cash deposits; at the same time there are 100,000 empty beds in the country, costing $2 billion to maintain.[5]

—The massive inequity between rich and poor is reflected in health statistics: infant mortality rates are 53% higher in poverty areas compared with nonpoverty areas, and people with lower incomes have higher rates of heart disease, high blood pressure, bronchitis, diabetes and other illnesses.[6] The life expectancy for Latino males in East Los Angeles is 55, compared with 72 for all male Californians.[7]

Not only does the American health system require full wallets in order to merit decent health care, but American-based transnational corporations, the absolute zenith of concentrated wealth and power, spread a massive toll of sickness and death around the globe.

—100,000 American workers die from work-related conditions each year and 4 million contract occupational diseases.[8] As the transnational corporations increasingly set up industrial plants in the poor nations, these same occupational hazards and death are exported around the world.[9]

—The American food industry has caused a deterioration of the American diet with the resultant epidemic of coronary artery disease.[10] That same food industry, aggressively expanding into poor nations, has been a key factor in the precipitous decline in breast feeding, resulting in greatly increased infant malnutrition.[11]

—The penetration of corporate agriculture for export into peripheral nations has evicted millions of small farmers from their lands and their livelihood and greatly reduced the land available for domestic crops, thereby creating massive unemployment, malnutrition and even starvation.[12]

The Need for a National Health Service

The American working class desperately needs a fully-funded national health service, or at the very least a federally-administered national health insurance program, to alleviate the grossest inequities of the health care system. With a national health service, the brutal denial of care to those without funds would come to a halt. Billions of dollars could be redirected from personal profit to community service by eliminating private insurance companies and by controlling the excess surgery, hospital beds and drugs.

As an example of a public national health insurance system, Canada delivers all basic medical services to the entire population at virtually no out-of-pocket cost. At the same time, Canada's health expenditures have risen far more slowly than those of the U.S. Administrative costs in Canada are only one-fourth those in the U.S.[13] As another example of a national health service, Great Britain similarly offers total care to everyone without out-of-pocket cost and has vastly increased the availability of health services to the British working class.

However, neither of these social reforms solves the most basic class inequities in the health sector. In Canada, physicians are holding the health system hostage by demanding large fee increases; if they don't get what they want, they "opt out" of the government health insurance and see rich private patients at higher fees.[14] This behavior is the first step in re-creating a 2-tier health system with long waits and inferior care for the working class that cannot afford private care.

The British national health service also reflects the enormous inequality between rich and poor. Members of the upper and upper-middle classes dominate the national health service's decision-making bodies. Consequently, national health service resources have been concentrated in the urbanized, wealthiest areas, leaving the poorer areas (where people are sicker) with inadequate services.[15] In addition, the Conservative Party is trying to cut national health service funds, which is one of the many ways the British working class is being forced to lower its standard of living under austerity capitalism.[16] Additionally, the limits of the national health service are seen in its incapacity to reduce the appalling burden of industrial accidents and illnesses that kill and maim the British working class just as they kill their American brothers and sisters.[17]

Though a national health service is badly needed and must be fought for to alleviate some of the suffering of the U.S. working class, it will not truly solve the inequities, the injustice and the unnecessary and global burden of death and disease wrought by capitalism itself. Only the struggle against the total domination of the transnational corporations—the struggle for a socialism in which the welfare of the majority takes precedence over the expansion of capital—can begin to address the vast differences between rich and poor, between educated and illiterate, between the rates of infant mortality, life expectancy, disability and death.

When the working class begins to make decisions—on the job, in the health clinics and hospitals, and throughout all levels of government—based on the needs of the majority rather than the profit rates of a tiny few, then the toll of occupational disease and death, of gruesome surgery without justification, and of needless drug-induced fatalities will begin to diminish. That is the society we must work for, a society in which the experts work for the people rather than take from the people, in which older people are treated equally as human beings rather than being discarded as worn-out machines. Only through the construction of a new society can the health system truly be repaired, because the health system is simply a part of and a reflection of the entire society.

A final note on health in the socialist countries: are these our models? We all know that health services are infinitely better in the USSR, in China and in Cuba than they were in the pre-revolutionary eras of these countries. We also know that these health services are far better than in comparable capitalist countries. Yet great imperfections exist in the health sectors of the socialist societies. All these countries were poor at the time of their revolutions, and by and large are still poor. The U.S. is wealthy, and socialist construction is far easier where scarcity is not so profound. In addition, the present socialist countries are constructing new societies in the midst of a capitalist world, and that hostile environment forces constant setbacks and compromises. The health systems of the socialist countries have solved the class inequities only to the extent that these countries have solved these inequities in general, and their records are still far from perfect. These countries are no model, but the vision with which their working classes fought is the vision for which we fight: an end to the sickness, despair and hopelessness that are such a constant by-product of capitalist production.

Marlene Dixon and
Thomas Bodenheimer M.D.

NOTES

1. "Health Care for All Americans Act" (Kennedy Bill), brochure, 1979.
2. Health Insurance Institute, *Source Book of Health Insurance Data, 1978-79.*
3. *Washington Post*, January 11, 1979 and March 1, 1980.
4. M. Silverman and P.R. Lee, *Pills, Profits and Politics* (Berkeley, University of California Press, 1974), pp. 264, 329.
5. *Los Angeles Times*, October 23, 1977. These statistics on unnecessary surgery, excess drugs and empty hospital beds are often used by the capitalist class to justify cutbacks in health services. We oppose the use of these statistics to deprive people of *needed* services, but the facts themselves speak to the human cost of medicine under capitalism.
6. N.A. Holtzman, "Prevention: Rhetoric and Reality," *International Journal of Health Services*, Vol. 9, No. 1, (1979), p. 31.
7. *Los Angeles Times*, December 7, 1979.
8. Vicente Navarro, "The Crisis of the Western System of Medicine in Contemporary Capitalism," *International Journal of Health Services*, Vol. 8, No. 2, (1978), p. 192.
9. R.H. Elling, "Industrialization and Occupational Health in Underdeveloped Countries" *International Journal of Health Services*, Vol. 7, No. 2, (1977), pp. 209-35.
10. Navarro, op. cit., p. 193.
11. D.B. Jelliffe and E.F.P. Jelliffe, "The Infant Food Industry and International Child Health," *International Journal of Health Services*, Vol. 7, No. 2, (1977), pp. 249-54.
12. T.S. Bodenheimer, "The Political Economy of Malnutrition: Generalizations from Two Central American Case Studies," *Archivos Latinoamericanos de Nutricion*, Vol. 22, (December 1972). pp. 495-506.
13. G.H. Hatcher, "Canadian Approaches to Health Policy Decisions – National Health Insurance," *American Journal of Public Health*, Vol. 68, (September 1978), pp. 881-89.
14. *Ottawa Citizen*, September 27, 1979.
15. Vicente Navarro, *Social Class, Policy Formation and Medicine: An Historical and Contemporary Analysis of the Medical Sector in Great Britain* (monograph), (1976), pp. 81, 94-96.
16. *Lancet*, October 20, 1979.
17. R.C. Clutterbuck, "The State of Industrial Ill-Health in the United Kingdom," *International Journal of Health Services*, Vol. 10, No. 1, (1980), pp. 149-160.

Class Struggle
in a
Beleaguered Health System

Thomas Bodenheimer

In recent years, a growing body of radical and Marxist literature has attempted to explain the workings of the U.S. health care system and the nature of the crisis within that system. Where many of these analyses have failed, however, has been in their grasp of the relationships binding the health care sector to the totality of U.S. monopoly capitalism. Academic medical centers, health insurance providers, and drug and hospital supply firms unquestionably exercise great influence over the delivery of health care in the U.S. today. The organized medical profession, though on the defensive, remains enormously influential. Yet none of these groups can wield their power or influence independently of the social forces that determine the direction of society as a whole. Rather than view the evolution of the health care system in the U.S. as the simple result of the pursuit of narrow interests by each of these institutions, an analysis of the changes in health care must begin from an understanding of the contradictions of contemporary capitalism. In order to understand the political and economic forces that are shaping the health care system in the contemporary U.S., we must begin with an examination of the principal classes in American society.

Classes in the U.S. Today

We can distinguish three principal classes in the contemporary U.S.: the bourgeoisie or capitalist class, the proletariat or working class and the petty bourgeoisie or middle class. Each of these classes in turn is composed of many different strata and subgroups, and the relations within these classes often manifest multiple contradictions. Yet, as we shall see, each of these three classes has a distinctive relation to the means of production which fundamentally determines its interests and its world outlook. It is the struggle among these classes which is the ultimate motive force behind the changes we shall examine in the U.S. health care system.

The Bourgeoisie

The capitalist class, or bourgeoisie, consists of the owners and controllers of the principal means of production and other units of economic activity: industrial and service corporations, banks and other financial institutions. Within this class, however, serious contradictions exist, many of which have important repercussions for the health system. One of the most important of these is the conflict between the monopoly sector (the large corporations which dominate most of the central industries of the U.S. economy and which operate together to control the market for their products) and the competitive sector (smaller firms which operate either on the periphery of the monopoly sector or in those industries which have not been subject to the overall process of concentration and centralization of capital). Within the U.S. bourgeoisie it is the monopoly sector which is the economically and politically decisive center of power.

The Proletariat

In direct opposition to the capitalist class stands the working class or proletariat. The working class includes all those who do not own or control means of production, and who must therefore sell their labor-power to the capitalist class in return for subsistence. The working class neither

2

controls the products it produces nor the labor process through which it produces them.

The U.S. working class has always been extremely heterogeneous. In addition to multiple divisions according to the nature of work (production, clerical, service, crafts, agricultural, sales, transportation, unemployed, etc.) the working class is subject to deep racial, national and sexual divisions.

As a portion of the U.S. population, the working class has grown significantly with the consolidation of monopoly capitalism and now makes up close to 80% of the population. This increase has primarily been at the expense of the self-employed farm population and other small proprietor strata. Yet in the past 25 years, major changes have taken place in its internal occupational structure which have radically transformed the nature of work of many American workers, and of the health work force in particular.

The most important of these changes has been the relative decline in the number of production workers and the accompanying increase in the clerical and service sectors. (1) This development is partially the result of the increased productivity of labor, brought about by the application in monopoly industry of increasingly complex labor-saving technology. The relative decline in the industrial working class as a portion of the U.S. proletariat gives capital a large relative surplus population for use in new areas of employment. One of these is the financial and administrative infrastructure, which has constituted a major source for the expansion of clerical employment. Another is those forms of service work which formerly, even under pre-monopoly capitalism, were done in the home by the family unit. Beginning with clothing production and food processing, monopoly capital has gradually taken over almost all of the former productive functions of the family. Braverman speaks of the results:

> ...the population no longer relies upon social organization in the form of family, friends, neighbors, community, elders, children, but with few exceptions must go to market and only to market, not only for food, clothing and shelter, but also for recreation, amusement, security, for the care of the young, the old, the sick, the handicapped. In time, not only the material and service needs but even the emotional patterns of life are channeled through the market. (2)

The tremendous expansion of the health system and of the numbers of health workers are one clear example of this process.*

The Petty Bourgeoisie

In addition to the two classes which form the central polarity of capitalist society, the bourgeoisie and the proletariat, there have always existed intermediate strata of various types throughout the history of capitalism. As Marx remarked about 19th century England: "Nevertheless, even here the stratification of classes does not appear in its pure form. Middle and intermediate strata even here obliterate lines of demarcation everywhere." (3) In the United States since the end of the 19th century, the concentration and centralization of capital has vastly reduced the size of the old petty bourgeoisie of independent proprietors. This class (farmers, small merchants, artisans, other small businessmen and self-employed professionals) has declined from being a majority of the U.S. population to a tiny fraction today. Much of this old petty bourgeoisie, especially small farmers, has since become part of the proletariat.

Yet the decline of the old petty bourgeoisie has not eliminated the middle strata which have complicated class analysis since Marx's time. The same process of economic concentration which destroyed the old small proprietor class has in turn given rise to a new petty bourgeois class. This class is principally composed of the managerial, professional and technical cadres required by the huge bureaucratic corporate and state organizations which have emerged with monopoly capitalism: managers, engineers, planners, consultants, program administrators, accountants, systems analysts, etc. The contradictory nature of the new petty bourgeois class derives from the fact that it takes on aspects of both the bourgeoisie and the proletariat.

Whereas the new petty bourgeoisie, like the proletariat, sells its labor-power to capital, there is a clear line of

---

*   These transformations in the occupational structure of the U.S. working class have also very much affected the nature of racial and sexual super-exploitation, and the antagonisms within the proletariat to which it gives rise. A full exploration of these developments is beyond our scope here. For an analysis of how these developments have transformed the oppression of women, and hence the struggle for women's emancipation, see Marlene Dixon, "Monopoly Capitalism and the Women's Movement," Synthesis Vol. I, No. 4.

demarcation between these two classes. The petty bourgeoisie exercises a substantial degree of control over its own labor process, and controls the labor process of the proletariat beneath it. This control, command and organization of the proletariat is indeed the specific function of the new petty bourgeois strata in monopoly capitalist society:

> Among these intermediate groupings are parceled out the bits of specialized knowledge and delegated authority without which the machinery of production, distribution and administration would cease to operate....Their conditions of employment are affected by the need of top management to have within its orbit buffer layers, responsive and "loyal" subordinates, transmission agents for the exercise of control and the collection of information, so that management does not confront unaided a hostile or indifferent mass. (4)

In addition, the salary levels of new petty bourgeois functionaries represent more than a simple exchange of labor-power for money; they represent a share in the surplus produced by the working class. Such pay differentials have the political function of binding the interests of the new petty bourgeoisie to the success of the corporate or state organizations in which they are employed and, ultimately, to the capitalist economy in which these institutions operate:

> Taking as our criteria the relation of functionaries within the capitalist system (be they middle-level corporate managers or professionals and managers in governmental, educational and health establishments) to the power and wealth that commands them against the masses of labor beneath them which they help to control, command and organize, there is no doubt that their greater loyalty is given first to themselves, secondly to the power and wealth that commands them, and not at all to the masses of labor beneath them. We do not, for that reason, count these "middle layers," functionaries and subaltern (subordinate) intellectuals, as part of the working class. (5)

Classes in the Health System

The three major classes we have discussed are all found in the health care sector; the changes in health institutions reflect the development of the class structure of U.S. society. The capitalist class has numerous interests in health care. First of all, many major corporations are engaged directly in the manufacture of health-related products for profit. Drug and hospital supply companies are among the most profitable businesses in the U.S. today. In addition, large corporations, in such diverse areas as food processing and electronics, are becoming increasingly involved in the manufacture of health-related equipment. Health insurance is a profitable endeavor for the largest life and other insurers in the U.S., and these companies are in turn closely tied to major banking and other financial institutions.

An important part of the health system consists of institutions that supposedly disavow the profit motive. Nonprofit community hospitals contain 70% of all acute-care hospital beds in the United States, and employ over two million workers. Yet these institutions do not function in substantially different ways from profit-making corporations. Columbia sociologist Amitai Etzioni writes: "...omissions, ambiguities and loopholes in the laws and regulations governing not-for-profit corporations presently make it possible for the trustees and staff of not-for-profit corporations to engage in a variety of financial practices which bring them personal profits over and above fees, salaries and fringe benefits due them for work performed." (6) A Health/PAC report puts the conclusion more bluntly: "Profit making in nonprofit hospitals is neither a policy choice nor a deviation by occasional crooks. It is a fundamental characteristic of the private business nature of the institution." (7) Most importantly, not-for-profit hospitals and other health facilities view expansion and growth as essential imperatives, in a way very similar to the competition among capitalist firms.

It is through the operation of not-for-profit hospitals and other health facilities that the banks have become involved in the health care system. Over the past two decades, many private hospitals have rebuilt and expanded competitively. As the traditional philanthropic sources of hospital capital funds have dried up, these hospitals have borrowed large sums for construction and equipment from major banks. The banks themselves have considered such lending as a good investment, especially since state governments have often guaranteed hospital loans. By 1976, every major private hospital in San Francisco, to name but one city, had become significantly indebted to a major bank. (8)

6

The Health Sector's Proletariat and Petty Bourgeoisie

Along with the expansion of the health care system in the U.S., the number of workers employed in health-related jobs has risen rapidly. In 1900 the health work force numbered about 330,000; in 1972 it stood at about 4.5 million overall. The largest part of this growth has taken place among workers in hospitals and similar facilities, increasing from 830,000 in 1946 to over 2.5 million in 1975. (9)

The health work force has also grown highly complex. A 1974 New York Blue Cross survey, for example, listed 280 non-physician job categories at its member hospitals. A plethora of new "allied health" occupations has developed, each claiming professional status for its members. More importantly, however, the organization of work in the hospital and other health settings has come to resemble increasingly the Taylorized organization of industrial production under monopoly capitalism:

> Hospitals deliver a qualitatively different product from that of manufacturing plants. Nevertheless, their labor structures demonstrate parallels with that of other industries. Hospital administrators have their counterparts in plant management, maintaining the operation and assigning the work force. Doctors as salaried employees of health institutions perform similarly to plant engineers in terms of their roles and responsibilities. Like engineers, doctors design the product and generally oversee the work process. Registered nurses, like shop foremen, supervise work at the point of production. Other nursing workers, directly providing patient care, are roughly comparable to skilled assembly line workers. It is they who are responsible for the day-to-day creation of the product. Finally, the unskilled institutional maintenance people (housekeeping, food service, and laundry) are not only drawn from the same labor pool as unskilled manufacturing workers, but do nearly interchangeable tasks. (10)

Numerous trends in the health system exemplify the evolution of the American petty bourgeoisie. Private, fee-for-service physicians are the major old petty bourgeois group in the health system, but they are on the decline. The growth of large-scale institutions with their requirements for managerial personnel has created a large new petty bourgeoisie in health as elsewhere in monopoly capitalist society. Increasing numbers of physicians are salaried by hospitals and play a managerial role. The growth of state involvement in health care has also led to the emergence of legions of health planners, policy analysts, program coordinators and similar technocrats in both federal and state governments and academic medical centers.

These changes have also transformed other health professions radically. The registered nurse, for example, is increasingly coming to be seen as an administrator, coordinator and supervisor of care provided by licensed practical nurses and other health workers. Hospital administrator has evolved from a rather minor caretaker role to an increasingly dominant role in hospital governance, often in a position of representing the federal government and other outside agencies in conflicts with hospital medical staffs. The expansion of allied health occupations has also led to the creation of new categories of licensed professions, all subordinate to the medical profession, which share many of the contradictory aspects of the new mass petty bourgeois occupations.

The Expansion of the Health System

The central contradiction between proletariat and bourgeoisie has ultimately been the determining force behind the evolution of the capitalist world economy and the political economy of the United States. It is the development of this contradiction since the 1930s that is responsible for the modern transformation of the U.S. health care system.

The development of class struggle in the monopoly industries of the U.S. provided an important stimulus for the post-World War II expansion of the health care system. This expansion had its roots in the growth of private health insurance. Health insurance became a mechanism by which money previously retained in the non-health sector of the economy was channeled to the health system, resulting in the expansion of hospitals, high-cost technology and increased numbers of health care personnel.

Private health insurance emerged out of the militancy of America's working people on the floors of the nation's largest factories during the 1930s. In early 1937, thousands of workers had taken over six General Motors plants, with supporting workers and wives outside protecting them against police action. Finally the company gave in and recognized the union. Thereafter, sit-down strikes blossomed across the country. Fearing a major class confrontation, monopoly capital conceded to union demands for collective bargaining and other rights and benefits. This concession was a major factor in the co-optation of U.S. unions, but also resulted in increased wages and benefits for monopoly sector workers, including health insurance. (11)

Following World War II, another wave of militant strikes swept the major monopoly industries: automobile, steel, rubber and others. Unions increasingly demanded that money be set aside to insure workers and their families against hospital costs. The number of people with health insurance, most of it collectively bargained, grew from 32 million in 1945 to 120 million in 1960. While the workers paid most of this money at first, later contracts increasingly stipulated that the employer would pay the insurance premium. About half the insurance bought by labor/capital bargaining was written by Blue Cross and Blue Shield, with the other half by commercial insurance companies such as Aetna, Metropolitan Life and Prudential.

The health insurance benefits won by unionized workers, however, were still not adequate protection against the financial impact of illness. Families with insurance still paid two-thirds of their medical bills out-of-pocket in the early 1960s. Policies frequently denied payment for pre-existing illnesses; the elderly were charged astronomical premiums through experience rating and other devices. These major gaps in health benefits led unions to join with retired workers to support the passage of government health insurance, first for the elderly in the form of Medicare. While the legislative battle for Medicare was a far cry from the militant sit-downs of the thirties, it was class struggle, simply in another form.

By pouring vast new sums into the health sector, Medicare and Medicaid furthered the expansion initiated by the spread of private insurance. In addition, these programs created the conditions for health institutions (especially hospitals) to inflate their prices massively, thereby pulling even more money into the health sector. Fully 53% of the new money pouring into the health system between 1965 and 1975 went for inflation rather than for more services to more people.

It was the growing strength of the U.S. economy that allowed industrial capitalists to support (or at least not to oppose) this vast expansion of health care financing. At the close of World War II, the United States was the only strong power in the world economy. Practically unscathed by the war, the U.S. held within its borders most of the productive potential of the industrialized world. MacMillan and Harris note that, shortly after the war, "The U.S., with six and one-half percent of the world's population, harvested one-third of the world's grain, half its cotton, smelted 55% of its steel and other basic metals, pumped 70% of the world's oil, used 50% of its rubber, generated 45% of its mechanical energy (and) produced 60% of its manufactured goods." (12) Where the productive capacities of the major rivals of the U.S. had survived the war, they were often inefficient and obsolete. The economic and political hegemony of the U.S. was almost total. Only such economic power could support a health system that grew over 1000% in 26 years, from $12 billion in 1950 to $139 billion in 1976.

Before World War II, the health care system had been largely an interaction between old petty bourgeois doctors and patients. By 1970, three factors had reduced this economic interaction to insignificance: the growth of private insurance, the expanded role of the state and the centrality of the hospital. 74% of health care dollars flowed through insurance companies and the government in 1975 compared to 32% in 1950. With insurance companies controlled by the bourgeoisie and with the government heavily influenced by the bourgeoisie, this change in financial relations enormously increased the potential power of the bourgeoisie in the health care sector. In addition, 48% of health care finances went to corporate health care institutions (hospitals and nursing homes) in 1975 compared to 16% in 1950; again, potentially increasing the power of the bourgeoisie at the expense of petty bourgeois doctors.

Thus the expansion of the health care system altered the balance of class forces within that system, with a consolidation of control over the delivery of health care by the capitalist class. In the context of an expanding economy in the 1950s and 1960s, there was little reason for monopoly capital or the bourgeois state to exercise its newly acquired influence in the health field; bourgeois control over the petty bourgeois doctors was largely a potentiality. With the subsequent crisis in U.S. capitalism, however, the bourgeoisie has moved to assert this control more definitively, with clear consequences for both the proletariat and petty bourgeoisie.

The Crisis of Capitalism and the Attack on Labor

Since the mid-1960s, the U.S. has declined from its position of dominance over the capitalist world economy, resulting in a worsening crisis of the domestic economy. (13) The crisis has been the consequence of tendencies toward stagnation inherent in monopoly capitalism, exacerbated by the very measures taken by the U.S. capitalist class to forestall the crisis and by the changes in the international position of the United States. As Alan Nasser notes, however, the confluence of these factors has meant that "monopoly capitalism has undergone a far-reaching structural transformation which has initiated an epoch of permanent crisis...chronic and indeed epochal in its implications." (14) This crisis, as we shall see, has led to a concerted attempt by the capitalist class to attack the standard of living of the proletariat. Both the crisis and the consequent attack on labor have had important effects on the development and expansion of health care institutions.

During the late 1960s, in a war-induced economic boom, the share of national income going to the working class increased significantly, while that going to the capitalist class fell. In 1965-66, total wages and salaries were 72.2% of the national income, but by 1969 they had risen to 76.3%. Corporate profits, on the other hand, dropped from 10.6% of national income to 8.2% over the same period. Thus the war-induced economic boom resulted in a significant profit squeeze. This was principally the result of a prolonged, war-generated period of low unemployment. The 1966-69 period was, in fact, the only time since World War II that unemployment was below 4% for such a sustained period of time.

With such a profit squeeze, the capitalist class tried to increase profits by raising prices. The inflation backfired, with the U.S. working class unable to buy the overpriced goods, and with cheaper foreign products increasingly moving into U.S. corporate markets both at home and abroad. By 1974, the capitalist class had understood that the limits on inflation had been reached, with higher prices meaning lower sales and profits.

As a consequence of the profit squeeze, the limits on inflation, and the weakening economic and political position of the U.S. in the post-Vietnam world, the U.S. bourgeoisie is mounting a sustained attack on the living standards of the proletariat in order to increase the rate of profit.

The Attack on Labor

The opening guns of the attack on labor were fired by Nixon's Phase II wage-price controls, implemented in November, 1971. This policy consisted of a strictly enforced freeze on wages, and a purely nominal freeze on prices, and thus allowed profits, interest and dividends to rise steadily. Largely as a result of Phase II, corporate profits soared. From the third quarter of 1972 (a year after Phase II was announced) until the second quarter of 1974 (the time of Nixon's resignation), after-tax wages rose by 8%, retail prices 16% and corporate profits 54%. (15)

The bourgeoisie did not list the attack on labor among the abuses of power for which Nixon was forced to resign. On the contrary, the attack was continued and refined under Ford. However, it did assume a new form, the planned recession. This was a clear attempt to use state intervention in the economy to keep unemployment high and thus wages low. The 9% official unemployment rate reached in 1975 shows the success of the engineered recession in the eyes of the bourgeoisie.

In his first several months in office, President Carter has shown that he intends to continue the assault on the working class's standard of living initiated by the Nixon-Ford administration. Like Ford, Carter has proclaimed inflation rather than unemployment to be the principal enemy, and his rescinding of the announced $50 tax rebate heralded a prolongation of the planned recession. Subsequently, administration stances on legislative issues have also come to resemble those of its predecessor. Carter's failure to support the $3 minimum wage and the common situs picketing bill, despite clear AFL-CIO backing, are just two examples of his anti-labor position. New tax breaks for corporations, the energy policy, cutbacks in social services and increased defense spending are other aspects of Carter's attack on labor. The rhetoric of sacrifice and "less is better than more" constitutes the ideological component of the attack on the working class.

In addition to federal intervention in the national economy to reduce the share of national income going to the proletariat, the attack on labor has taken several other forms. One such manifestation is the runaway shop – in which capital closes productive facilities in relatively high-wage areas and relocates in either low-wage, non-union areas of the United States (right-to-work states such as Nevada and Colorado, for example), or to peripheral and semi-peripheral countries abroad where repressive regimes serve to keep working class wages at starvation levels. Even where such moves never actually take place, the threat of a runaway shop can often contain workers' demands for higher wages, or force them to take cuts in order to keep their jobs. "Productivity" campaigns (speedups) have also been an important strategy of the capitalist attack.

The Attack on Labor and the Health System

As a result of collective bargaining, the basic monopoly industries (auto, steel, electrical, etc.) have been forced to pay for the health care of their workers. As inflation in the health sector is running far above inflation in the economy as a whole, these industries are forced to pay more and more for their workers' health care. General Motors now complains that it puts out more money for employee health benefits than for steel to build its cars. Ford Motor Company spent $298 million on health insurance in 1975, four times the total of ten years ago. (16)

Since rising health care costs cut into corporate profits, a reduction in the costs of employees' health care is one mechanism the monopoly capitalists are pursuing in order to ease their profit squeeze and lessen the crisis in capitalism. In addition, the bourgeoisie is working to cut governmental health budgets as a means to reduce their taxes, to lower the inflationary effects of governmental health spending, and to generally attack the living standard of working people.

But the attack on labor in the health sector not only affects the working class. In fact, the attack on labor in the health sector has turned into a general attack on the entire health sector. The moves of the bourgeoisie and the bourgeois state against the health system constitute, and in turn have unleashed, the heightening of class contradictions: within the bourgeoisie, between the bourgeoisie and the petty bourgeoisie, within the petty bourgeoisie and between the petty bourgeoisie and the working class.

The Assault on the Working Class

The fundamental characteristic of the attack on the health sector is an assault on the working class, both directly and indirectly (through the state). In the direct attack, corporations have begun to demand that workers assume larger portions of their health insurance premiums, formerly paid by the corporations themselves. This was a recent issue in automobile contract negotiations and is likely to emerge as a major point of contention in other industries as well. Another tactic is to reduce the amount of care an employee is allowed to obtain. Goodyear Tire has created peer-review programs in Ohio and Illinois to monitor the number of days their employees stay in the hospital. The program has cut an entire day off the average length of stay of company employees, at a savings to Goodyear of $100 per patient day. Similar programs are being planned by Proctor and Gamble, Greyhound and Caterpillar Tractor. Other employers, for example General Mills and Uniroyal, have been looking into the creation of health maintenance organizations such as the Kaiser plan, which provide care which is cheaper in part because it is so inaccessible that employees can't get doctor appointments when they need them. (No doubt it is true that many people receive too much health care: excess surgery, over-hospitalization and unnecessary prescriptions, and a reduction in these excesses is not an attack on the working class. But it is clear that reductions in essential services have been and will continue to be just as frequent or more frequent than reductions in unnecessary services. In that way, the campaign against unnecessary surgery and hospitalization becomes a cover for the attack on labor.)

The actions of the bourgeois-controlled state have been far more important than direct bourgeois action in the attack on labor in the health system. Until the early 1970s, most federal health policy was determined by the bourgeoisie and petty bourgeoisie in the health sector: drug company executives, the insurance industry, private hospitals and the AMA. With the crisis in capitalism, the bourgeoisie in the non-health sectors of the economy has begun to intervene in federal health policy with the aim of reducing governmental contributions to health financing. Thus far the major thrust has been the attempts of the Nixon and Ford administrations to drastically cut back the Medicare and Medicaid programs. Many of these cuts did not go through Congress (where the bourgeoisie and petty bourgeoisie of the health sector still wield a great deal of power), but increasingly, Congress is expected to go along with the executive branch in approving cutbacks. As Senator Herman Talmadge of the Senate Finance Committee health subcommittee stated, "There is no way that health-care financial cost increases of the magnitude that have occurred will be tolerated in the future." (17) Already, programs instituted in the 1960s in such areas as prevention and neighborhood clinics have been cut substantially.

Thus far, cutbacks at the state and local levels have been many times more brutal than federal cutbacks. State contributions to Medicaid programs are being cut severely in many parts of the country. In California, a series of cutbacks culminated in the 1971 Medi-Cal reform legislation, which substantially increased the contribution of county governments to local public hospitals and thus accelerated the trend towards their closure. Similar cutbacks in New York State had begun as early as 1968.

Such reductions in state contributions have worsened the already tenuous state of municipal and county hospitals in both rural and urban areas throughout the country. In California, for example, county hospitals are being closed, sold to private corporations, or transferred to university auspices. In counties where they have not been closed or transferred, such as Los Angeles and San Francisco, aggressive new billing and other policies have been instituted, making county hospital billing practices little different from those of private facilities. Last year, for example, San Francisco announced stringent new billing policies for its county hospital, effectively eliminating county-financed free care at the institution.

New York City's fiscal crisis has led to the closing of several municipal hospitals and to severe staffing cutbacks at those remaining open. Similar closures and cutbacks have now occurred, or threaten to take place, in Boston, Philadelphia, Chicago and other cities. Dr. Russell Nelson, chairman of the Commission on Public General Hospitals, recently stated that decisions made "not by the logic of public policy, but in hasty response to financial crisis," were threatening the future of these institutions nationwide, and cited state Medicaid cutbacks as a major contributing factor. (18) The toll such closures and cutbacks will take on the health and lives of working people in the U.S. is incalculable.

In particular, then, the largely non-unionized and uninsured competitive sector workers and the enlarging reserve army are hit hard by the bourgeois offensive against the health system, with the cutbacks of public hospitals and Medicaid. And, as all hospitals come under increasing attack from the bourgeoisie, hospital workers (who constitute a part of the competitive sector labor force) are being hit by speedups, layoffs and degradation and Taylorization of their jobs.

Contradictions Among the Bourgeoisie

In the health care arena, the major contradiction within the capitalist class is between those who, on the one hand,

15

have been forced by collective bargaining to pay into the health system, and those who, on the other hand, profit from supplying, insuring or delivering health care. The latter applaud the increasing percentage of the GNP going into health; the former deplore it. In one sense, it is oversimplified to separate the health and non-health bourgeoisie, since the interlocks between the one and the other are so great. Drug companies are now multi-product conglomerates, insurance companies insure and invest in many things besides health care, banks lend to every conceivable corporation, not just to hospitals.

Despite these complexities, it is undeniable that the bourgeois attack on its brethren in the health sector is taking place. One of the more dramatic examples was the closing down of a number of small corporate prepaid health plans for Medicaid patients in Southern California. These health plans were ripping off, rather than saving money for, the state and federal Medicaid program. The struggle against the prepaid health plans, as well as against some for-profit nursing homes in California, included multiple investigations and hearings for fraud, firings of top government officials and great publicity; but behind the fireworks was the determination of the bourgeois-backed state to reduce the costs of Medicaid against the maneuverings of health-related businesses to make a fast buck.

Less dramatic but far more important are the moves of corporations and the state against hospitals. With hospital costs accounting for 40% of the health care dollar and causing much of the health care inflation, corporate attempts to reduce the costs of care would naturally focus on the hospitals. One example of a direct attack took place in Phoenix, Arizona, where the city's largest employer, Motorola, entered into a confrontation with the Good Samaritan hospital chain which cares for many of Motorola's employees. Motorola published full page ads listing all the ways in which the hospital wasted money and pushed hard for a slowing down of the yearly rate increases.

Another mechanism the bourgeoisie is using to attack the health care businesses is through governmental health planning. In 1974, Congress passed the National Health Planning and Resource Development Act, which authorized the creation of a network of regional Health Systems Agencies to review and, if necessary, block hospital expansion and equipment purchases. In most parts of the United States the implementation has been slow, in part due to opposition by the medical profession. The HSA concept has been successful, however, in those areas where HSAs have had the backing of monopoly corporations. Goodyear Tire, for example, has six managers on HSA committees in the Akron, Ohio, area where it is headquartered. With Goodyear's backing, the HSA pressured local hospitals to stop construction of additional maternity units and in fact succeeded in closing one maternity facility entirely. The United States Chamber of Commerce and General Motors Corporation have also urged executives to participate in HSAs. (19)

In addition to the bourgeois attack, with the assistance of Ralph Nader and other "consumerists," on the proliferation of hospital beds and specialty units, both the federal government and nine states have attempted to regulate hospital rates directly. The clearest example was Nixon's wage-price controls, which hit hospitals very hard; unlike most non-health businesses, hospitals were strictly limited in their price increases during the years of the controls. The most significant action of the Carter administration in the health field has been the proposed Hospital Cost Containment Act, which would limit increases in hospital revenues to 9% in the first year (compared to hospital cost increases of 15% in 1976 and a probable 15% in 1977). Hospitals are dead set against the legislation; the lines are drawn.

The Bourgeoisie vs. the Petty Bourgeoisie

But the attack on hospitals signifies more than simply an intercapitalist split, for the hospitals themselves contain an internal class contradiction. Many non-profit hospital boards have begun to move against the class that most clearly demands and profits from the excess hospital beds and specialty units, the petty bourgeois doctors. Thus we see the growing class conflict within the hospital itself, the escalating war between governing board and medical staff, with the administrators, formerly tools of the physicians, becoming increasingly tied to the corporate hospital board. The doctors are beginning to fight back against the encroachment by the board on what they consider to be their turf, on the question, for example, of whether the hospital administration, speaking for the board, has the power to grant and revoke staff privileges, a power previously in the hands of the medical staff. The physicians' journal, Medical Economics, ran an article in 1977 entitled "Our Enemy — The Hospital," and another a few years ago, "Does the Administration Hold All the Cards?"

The doctors see the bourgeoisie coming down on them in many different ways: through the government, hospitals, planning agencies, insurance companies and the media. Each attack is designed to reduce the flow of money from corporate or governmental coffers to the petty bourgeois doctors by cutting fees, reducing hospitalization, curbing excess surgery or charging more for malpractice insurance. In many cases, the doctors, being too weak to fight back against the bourgeoisie and behaving in classic petty bourgeois fashion, shift their losses onto the working class.

The doctors see the government as their main enemy. Since 1971, federal administrations have favored health maintenance organizations (HMOs) which would reduce doctors' power, freedom of action and probably their income. In its 1973 report, the Committee for Economic Development, one of the most influential big business groups advising the government, pushed for HMOs. Doctors are increasingly aware that big business is against them. One Medical Economics article is headlined "Are Our Business Friends Deserting Us?" and a more recent article, called "Big Business and You: More Intervention Ahead," discusses how business increasingly supports the HMO concept. The AMA recently made a strong public criticism of the corporate New York Times for running a major series on excess surgery and medical incompetency.

In 1972, Congress passed a requirement for peer review over physicians' practices, designed (albeit ineffectively) to cut down on excess treatments. The federal government has placed limits on Medicare fees, and both the federal and various state governments have reduced Medicaid fees. These fee limitations provide a classic example of the infuriated petty bourgeois, wildly gesticulating against the bourgeois state while actually shifting their losses onto the working class. The Union of American Physicians rhetoricizes, "Which of these straws will break your back, doctor? Will it be mandatory fee ceilings that strangle your take-home pay while inflation continues to gnaw away at you?" Yet what actions do the doctors take? With Medicare fee limits, the doctors started to bill patients for their services, forcing the patients to collect a portion of the total fee from the federal government. The doctors ended up with whatever fee they wanted, and the government paid the Medicare patient less. Thus the doctors turned the Medicare fee restrictions into higher costs for their patients. With Medicaid, doctors aren't allowed to bill patients, but must collect from Medicaid directly. In the case of Medicaid fee cuts, large numbers of doctors simply refused to see Medicaid patients at all, since they get more from private insurance and Medicare. The effect for Medicaid patients, who form the most marginal sector of the proletariat, has been disastrous. In some rural counties, there are no obstetricians or pediatricians at all who will see Medicaid patients, and even in the cities care is often restricted to high-volume, low-quality Medicaid mills or overcrowded, decaying public hospitals.

The antagonism of petty bourgeois doctors to the government, the hospital board, the HMO, the HSA and peer review are perfectly understandable. But the class contradictions have really peaked when doctors turn against the very institution they created: Blue Shield. Blue Shield plans were created in the 1940s by state medical societies to ensure that private insurance would be controlled by the doctors themselves, thus guaranteeing the maintenance of high fees. However, the bourgeois class interests of Blue Shield executives and managers (to take in more money than they pay out) are coming into conflict with the petty bourgeois class interests in Blue Shield (to pay out as much money in doctor fees as possible), and Blue Shield management is turning against the doctors. A recent California Medical Association convention seriously debated a resolution to condemn California Blue Shield (which is controlled by the California Medical Association itself) for cutting fees. In July 1977, the Massachusetts Federation of Physicians and Dentists filed a class action suit against Blue Shield of Massachusetts and called for Blue Shield's dissolution because of cuts in physician fees.

The malpractice crisis of 1975 was another instance of class struggle between the bourgeoisie and the petty bourgeoisie, with the bourgeois insurance companies winning out and the petty bourgeois doctors shifting their crisis onto the working class. The insurance industry raised malpractice premiums to unprecedented heights, with increases as great as 500% in a year, to cope with the growing size and number of malpractice awards, and also to offset stock market losses related to the general crisis in capitalism. Physicians throughout California went on strike, first in the Bay Area, later in Los Angeles. The effect was no victory at all for the doctors, but the layoff of thousands of hospital workers and the denial of health care to tens of thousands of working class patients. More importantly, physician fees have skyrocketed to make working class patients pay the costs of higher malpractice premiums. During the malpractice crisis there was also vicious name-calling between the two involved petty bourgeois groups, the doctors and the lawyers. Finally, the long-term solution to the malpractice problem in many states is the passage of "tort reform" legislation, which is legislation to make it far harder for patients to successfully sue incompetent doctors and to reduce the malpractice settlements that successful suits bring: again, the solution finally worked out between the doctors and the bourgeoisie is a direct attack on the working class.

Conclusion

The class struggle in the contemporary U.S. health care system – the closing of public hospitals, the attack by insurance companies on physicians, the moves by the federal government and private corporations to cut health care costs, the howls of private physicians against the hospital boards and planning agencies – forms a part of the class contradictions of U.S. society as a whole. These class contradictions are rooted in the fundamental polar antagonism between the proletariat and the bourgeoisie. The form of this antagonism has shifted from the sit-downs of the 1930s, which because of U.S. world hegemony could be co-opted into collective bargaining and temporary economic gains, to the increasing brutality of the attack on labor stemming from the world crisis of capitalism. As we have seen, the forces leading to the tremendous expansion and subsequent moves toward contraction of the health system have been rooted in the earlier expansion and current crisis of U.S. monopoly capitalism.

We cannot understand the health system without understanding the entire economy of which it is but one sector, for the health system is in truth no integral system at all. No analysis of the health sector in isolation is of any value because it does not reflect reality. And similarly, we cannot presume to change the health system to the benefit of the masses of people without engaging in the overall class struggle of the proletariat against the bourgeoisie's attack on labor. Discussions of reform or of revolutionary change confined to the health system are pure fantasy.

Whereas the health sector can only be understood in its larger social context, the class contradictions within the health sector are helpful in understanding class behavior in society as a whole. For example, the behavior of the petty bourgeois physicians when under attack by the bourgeoisie should strike from our minds any thought of class alliance of the proletariat and the petty bourgeoisie against the capitalist class. The doctors are again proving the universality of the political behavior of the petty bourgeoisie as a class: when the going gets rough, stomp all over those below you. Only the proletariat, with nothing to lose and everything to gain, has interests which correspond to the emancipation of all humankind.

NOTES

1. Harry Braverman, Labor and Monopoly Capital (New York, Monthly Review Press, 1974), p. 379.
2. Ibid., p. 276.
3. Karl Marx, "The Process of Capitalist Production as a Whole," Capital, Vol. III (New York, International Publishers, 1972), p. 885.
4. Braverman, op. cit., p. 406; see also Marlene Dixon, "Proletarian versus Petty Bourgeois Socialism," Synthesis, Vol. I, No. 1 (Summer, 1976), p. 5.
5. Dixon, op. cit., p. 5.
6. Amitai Etzioni and Pamela Doty, "Profit in Not-For-Profit Institutions," Philanthropy Monthly, February, 1976, p. 22.
7. Health Policy Advisory Center, The Profit in Nonprofit Hospitals, San Francisco, 1976, p. 10.
8. David Landau, "Trustees: The Capital Connection," Health/Pac Bulletin, No. 74 (January-February, 1977), p. 15.
9. Barbara Caress, "Health Manpower: Bigger Pie, Smaller Pieces," Health/PAC Bulletin, No. 62 (February, 1975), p. 8.
10. Ibid.
11. James O'Connor, The Fiscal Crisis of the State (New York, St. Martin's Press, 1973), p. 22.
12. In The American Takeover of Britain (1968), quoted by Sidney Lens, The Forging of The American Empire (New York, Crowell, 1971), p. 337.
13. See Joyce Kolko, America and the Crisis of World Capitalism (Boston, Beacon Press, 1974), pp. 1-28.
14. Alan Nasser, "The Twilight of Capitalism: Contours of the Emerging Epoch," The Insurgent Sociologist, Vol. VI, No. 2 (Winter, 1976), p. 8.
15. Ibid., p. 11.
16. Jerry Bishop, "Medical Advances and the Growth of Insurance Dim Hopes of Curbing Rising Health Care Costs," Wall Street Journal, February 17, 1977, p. 30; Arlene Hershman, "The Race to Cut Medical Costs," Dun's Review, May, 1977, p. 48.
17. Hershman, op. cit., p. 48.
18. Washington Report on Medicine and Health, April 11, 1977, p. 4.
19. Hershman, op. cit., p. 52.

Workers' Report on the Conditions of Labor and Their Effect on Patient Care at San Francisco General Hospital

This is a unique case study of the problems at SFGH. Unlike most professional studies, the *Report* was initiated by SFGH workers themselves and it is filled with their voices. From every department of the hospital, workers express their frustration with inhuman working conditions. As a very result of those conditions, they cannot provide the high-quality care that they know patients deserve.

The *Report* does not stop with workers' dissatisfaction, or with the situation at a single hospital. It also explains why SFGH has so many problems: both public workers and the consumers of public services are abused through irresponsible budget cutbacks, incompetent city management, and the constant pressure to transform a public service institution into a profit-making enterprise. Finally, the *Report* presents a proposal to remedy the situation; it is a *call to action.*

By the Institute for the Study of Labor and Economic Crisis with the assistance of the Workers Committee to Improve Hospital Services and Rebel Worker Organization.

Order from:
Synthesis Publications
2325 Third Street
Suite 415-F
San Francisco, CA 94107
(415) 626-4483

42 pages
Price: $2.00 plus $.50 postage for orders under $5.00; add 10% to orders over $5.00. California residents add 6% sales tax (6½% in BART counties).

The Limits of Reformism

Community-Worker Control and the 'Dellums Bill'

This article is one of the very few treatments of U.S. health care reform programs from the viewpoint of Marxist class analysis. Such an analysis is essential to understand past and present developments in the health sector, and to predict the effects of proposed future reforms. Our analysis finds that even the farthest-reaching reforms are incapable of truly lifting the burden of poor health that weighs so heavily on the U.S. working class. In this sense, we have described the "limits" of reformism.

This is not to say that we should withhold support from such short-range health reform measures as the Kennedy national health insurance bill or the Dellums national health service proposal. We can never forget the barbaric cruelty of the U.S. health system which day after day denies health care to millions of working class people because they are unable to pay. We do need a national health program that will alleviate the worst of this brutality.

Yet to think of these reform measures as real solutions is a serious error, an error that can lead health reformers to a sense of disappointment, frustration and betrayal. Our class analysis serves to place these reforms in a larger perspective, so that we always keep in mind what we can win and what we will always lose as long as we accept the limitations and bondage imposed on the majority of Americans by capitalism itself. Ultimately, the working class must tear those bonds asunder and bring forth a new era in which all can equally enjoy full, healthy and productive lives.

Editors

The Limits of Reformism

Community-Worker Control and the 'Dellums Bill'

Barbara Bishop M.D. and

Thomas Bodenheimer M.D.

 During the past decade various sectors of the bourgeoisie have proposed plans for national health insurance. These have ranged from the Kennedy-Griffiths Bill, which would finance all medical expenses through Social Security and income taxes, to proposals by Nixon and Ford which would provide federal subsidies to private insurance companies. All of these plans were spurred by concern on the part of the capitalists to control the mounting costs of health care, a major contributor to the rate of domestic inflation, while at the same time providing a state subsidy for the continually soaring profits of the health care industry. None of these proposals offered any significant alteration in the delivery of health care.

In 1971 the Medical Committee for Human Rights (MCHR), a national organization of the New Left health movement, drafted an alternative to the Kennedy Bill, based on the desire to eliminate profit from health care. It proposed a delivery apparatus composed of neighborhood-based "community-worker controlled" health centers. In early 1974 Rep. Ron Dellums (D., Calif.) expressed interest in sponsoring such a national health plan in Congress. MCHR's original conception, translated into legislation, has come to be known as the "Dellums Bill." Not yet introduced into Congress, the bill calls for the establishment of a National Community Health Service (NCHS), based on a progressive income tax on individuals and corporations.

Many people who consider themselves socialists have lined up behind the "Dellums Bill" as their vision of socialist health care in the U.S. However, those of us committed to the struggle for proletarian hegemony must ask the question: Socialism for whom? We propose in this article to analyze the class character of the "Dellums Bill" in light of its proposals for "community" and "worker" control, reforms which are widely promoted as ideals among the social-democratic left. In the context of the current epoch of massive attacks against the standard of living of the working class we will examine what such petty bourgeois "reforms" mean in the struggle for proletarian socialism.

Proposals for community control grew out of demands for black power (and later Chicano and Native American power), which were actualized by demonstrations, sit-ins, riots and takeovers. The autonomous power of people in revolt was established in the very act of struggle and nurtured the growth of revolutionary consciousness in the very act of participation in collective struggles. The response by the bourgeoisie to these actions was to offer various forms of community participation, such as the advisory boards established by OEO in neighborhood health centers. These OEO "Demonstration Projects" were specifically targeted at those communities where there had been demonstrations.

As we will show, such schemes of community participation resulted not in cooptive concessions (i.e., compromises to the right) but in the further consolidation of petty bourgeois control over community service resources. Pressures to become "good administrators" and "responsible citizens" petty-bourgeoisified and liquidated whatever class-conscious proletarian forces were developing within these community groups.

Workers' Control – The Exercise of Class Power

It is no accident that such a "legitimate" schema for workers' self-management is put forward at this time:

25

demands for workers' control are heightening in Europe, spontaneous struggles are flourishing in U.S. workplaces and militancy is rising among health workers. Andre Gorz states it well:

> When we speak about workers' control we usually have some very different things in mind. Some see workers' control as an end in itself, i.e., as something that can and must be won within the framework of the capitalist system, to improve the situation of the working class. Others look at workers' control as something that will never be won as long as capitalism exists, and that must be championed for precisely that reason....workers' control is not an end in itself. It is mainly a means or method, a means whose true significance can be understood only if we place it in a strategic perspective of social and political revolution. (1)

We must understand these demands in the context of the crisis in the world capitalist system, a product of the current epoch of advanced monopoly capitalism. Since 1966 full employment of productive resources has led to a severe squeeze on corporate profits. In order to maintain their rate of profit, monopoly capitalists have inflated prices, at the same time cutting back on production (stagflation). Economies of the advanced capitalist countries have become synchronized due to the activities of the multinationals and the interconnections of state and world fiscal and monetary policies. This combination of factors has resulted in a historically unprecedented crisis, to which the capitalists have responded with a systematic assault on the working class in the U.S., via Nixon's wage controls and Ford's planned recession. Forced unemployment keeps wages down while inflated prices jack profits up and cut further into real wages. The scenario of prolonged "austerity capitalism" has been combined with exhortations about "belt-tightening" and "lowered expectations." No longer, we are told, should a worker assume he can better his position in life, save a little for a bigger house or send his children to school. Current collective bargaining agreements promise at best to keep wages indexed to inflation or to make up a portion of what was lost due to inflation during the life of the last contract.

In prior times the working class could act on the assumption that there were heaps of ready cash in the corporations' bank accounts. Job actions were based on the premise that the employer, if pressed hard enough, would eventually give in and grant higher wages and better working conditions. However, the increasing complexity of advanced monopoly capital has replaced this flexibility with rigid planning of production. Thus:

- –The quickened pace of technological innovation calls for advance planning of the corporation's future investment.
- –The greater weight of fixed capital compels long-term financial planning of amortization, depreciation, reserves and financial costs.
- –Increased international competition prevents unforeseen higher costs from being offset by higher prices.
- –Rigid financial planning also calls for rigid predetermination of labor costs. (2)

Within such a system unplanned labor demands jeopardize the corporation's financial planning and are considered a direct attack on the logic and balance of capitalism.

Thus, if we fight very hard, we may win more than the corporations planned for us to have. However, our experience has taught us to expect one of two responses: 1) the company will run away to a foreign dictatorship, where labor costs are greatly reduced compared to the U.S. and control of labor "unrest" is enforced by U.S. military aid; or 2) the company will restore its rate of profit by hiking prices, by speedups and layoffs and by rationalized work processes to further intensify the work and cheapen wages. Thus the working class is made to pay dearly for what small gains it has won.

In the context of such despotic management, workers have come to understand that unless they win direct control over the labor process, they cannot prevent the capitalists' taking with one hand what they grant with the other. Again to quote Gorz:

> Genuine workers' control is something quite intolerable to capitalist management, however enlightened it may pretend to be, because genuine workers' control attacks at its very source the domination and exploitation of labor by capital. (3)

Fundamentally, the struggle for workers' control is a struggle for power, power exercised by the working class as a class-for-itself. This struggle can be waged effectively only if the working class demonstrates in itself the capacity for exercising power over the process of production. Thus the auto workers in Italy actualized their demands for workers' control by checkerboard strikes. Tire workers in Turin organized direct shop actions to vary the work speeds in order to prove their capacity to run the factory and abolish piece rates. Health workers in New York City took over and operated a neighborhood clinic in their struggle to address their own community's health needs. In these instances workers did not demand control as something that could be granted by management. They struggled by simply taking control of the factory or shop and by making it function their way. As many of us learned in the civil rights movement, control is not something we can ask for and be given. It is something we have to take and it will only be "granted" because we have taken it already and won't give it up.

Worker Participation — Bourgeois Democracy in Action

Liberal bourgeois ideologues have borrowed a great deal from European examples of social-democratic "worker self-determination." We can draw our own lessons and apply them to the historically co-opted nature of the U.S. trade union movement.

The idea of worker participation in management dates back to the pre-World War I period when the modern labor movement had its beginning in Germany. In large part a response to demands by radicals within and outside the trade union movement, the resulting legal framework for "democratization of the economy" was clearly motivated by both management and trade union opposition to the radicals' demand to place executive power over production in the hands of the rank-and-file works councils. The modern German version of co-determination arose following World War II, with the rebuilding of German corporate enterprises, the consolidation of the German state, and the passing of the Co-Determination Act covering the iron, steel and mining industries.

The trade unions often draw a parallel between economic co-determination and political democracy, a parallel that is justified only in the sense of bourgeois parliamentary politics. Their goals are the same — the manipulation of the masses of people by a ruling elite, under the guise of "consent of the governed." Co-determination as viewed by the German Trade Union Federation (DGB) is not aimed to eliminate capitalist power and establish working class hegemony, but rather to rationalize existing class relations. As the DGB has itself stated, "A general conception of co-determination of this type pre-supposes a system of free enterprise based on the principle of free market economy." (4) The DGB has little interest in challenging class relations, for it has struck a bargain with the ruling class: in return for the consolidation of its petty bourgeois managerial position and the extension of co-determination to all industry, the DGB offers the consent of the workers to operate within the limits of capitalist society.

Submission by the German trade unions to the role of the state in economic planning and their support for the ruling Social Democratic Party (SPD) during the late fifties and early sixties resulted in the following, as described by a German author:

> The classical workers' movement, solidarity of the trade unions in defense of the workers' interests, and the use of the strike as their ultimate weapon is dead. The reformist workers' movement was no match for the carrot and stick approach of the new capitalism, which, aided by state intervention, rearmament, planned obsolescence, the oppressive use of technology in relation to its limited social possibilities, imperialist expansion and finally, by the widespread introduction of social welfare, has been able temporarily to avert its impending crisis, with relatively full employment and controlled growth. What is left of the old trade union movement is a system of structures reduced to insurance agencies which offer the workers a slice of the pie of capitalist "social progress".... To the extent that trade union struggles under those conditions still take place, they resemble maneuvers staged by some high command whose result is fixed at an office desk rather than democratic resistance movements; and often they only act as a release of accumulated dissatisfaction. (5)

So much for their works councils and employee-chosen labor directors. The same author comments on this sorry state of affairs:

> Social dictatorship in neocapitalism does not need to coincide in each case with terrorism and formal

destruction of the workers' movements or with suppression of every special interest representation of the workers. It need only insure that the latter submit their economic and sociopolitical behavior to the needs of capitalist production, and that they respect this predetermined framework. (6)

Let's examine Sweden, the dream world of welfare state reformism. For the workers:

Intensification of production, close supervision, and discipline have been the consequences of this development for workers and lower grades of office employees. A fast-growing corps of technologists and economists, under orders from the capitalists, is carrying out increasingly inhumane work studies. The volume of work submitted to such treatment has trebled over the last decade. The wage system has been made more complex and, as a result, more difficult for workers to check on. This in turn has worked against efforts to have demands made at local negotiations met. Local strikes are forbidden by law, and fully fifteen years have passed since the Swedish Federation of Trade Unions has called an official strike. The introduction of a technically advanced production system has resulted in the subordination of safety considerations to the demands of the profit motive, and unsanitary and demoralizing jobs are becoming increasingly common. Over eighty per cent of the Federation's members believe that their jobs involve health risks. In addition, many older workers will face the threat of redundancy in the 1970's because they are no longer regarded as "profitable propositions." (7)

For the capitalists:

By means of investment strikes, dismissal of workers, closure of companies, and the movement of capital abroad, the capitalists can sabotage the government's attempts to implement Socialist policies. The government's reluctance to introduce capitalist levies, to nationalize strategic sectors of the economy and land, and directly to intervene in matters relating to company policy, shows they are afraid of retaliatory action on the part of big business. Every attempt to follow through economic policies which are wholly rational from the point of view of the majority but inimical to the interests of the capitalists is invariably greeted with a howl of indignation from the bourgeois press: "State interference!" they cry, and "Abuse of power!" (8)

Collective bargaining is reduced to a yearly negotiation between the Swedish Employers' Confederation (SAF) with 25,000 members, the Swedish Federation of Trade Unions (LO) encompassing 1.6 million industrial workers and the Central Organization of Salaried Employees (TCO) representing 50% of Sweden's white-collar employees. This industrial peace, applauded throughout the capitalist world, is directly related to the highly centralized collaboration between labor, management and the state.

The agents of collaboration, the chief proponents of the Swedish social-democratic neo-capitalist state, the executioners of this grand plan, are the petty bourgeois technocrats: in relation to bourgeois interests these technocrats function as subalterns in the regimentation of the labor force, while they simultaneously pursue their own petty bourgeois class interests as mediated through the semi-independent instrumentality of the state.

Nationalized Health Care — Who Benefits?

In the U.S. the petty bourgeois social democrats are not as consolidated in their power, but it is the radicals from this "new" petty bourgeoisie, the technocrats and managers, that generate Nader's Raiders, that champion the Occupational Safety and Health Act, that back nationalized health care proposals like the "Dellums Bill." Operating out of their own class interest, the radical petty bourgeoisie refuses to recognize that nationalization of industry per se, as with all forms of state capitalist intervention in private enterprise, does not necessarily hold benefit for the proletariat, but on the contrary, can further constrict the ability of the working class to take action in its own interests.

Nationalization, like power, is no longer today...an end in itself: to achieve it there must be a struggle, but before there can be a struggle it must be clear toward what end nationalization is the means. (9)

Nationalization, instead of changing power relations and

opening up a breach in the capitalist system, can strengthen this system. For example, a neo-capitalist government, in purchasing a poorly profitable industry, can render a service to its present owners by permitting them to invest their capital in more profitable industries.

The health industry is at present very profitable, especially among drug and hospital supply corporations and insurance companies. The delivery of health services has to date not been profitable directly, since most hospitals are run as not-for-profit agencies. However, capital from hotel management and stockholding companies has been flowing into the field of hospitals and, through scientific management, may increase their profitability. While the rapid inflation in health costs (nearly doubling the rate of inflation in the general economy) benefits the hospital and insurance industries, it also contributes to rising costs for monopoly capital due to the increasing cost of maintenance of the labor force. Monopoly capital demands monopoly labor, in order to guarantee steady production and a disciplined work force, but in return the trade unions demand contract benefits such as health insurance. As the costs of health care mount, the portion of real wages eaten up by health benefits expands, thus limiting gains that monopoly labor can win at the bargaining table. Therefore, a nationalized health system, which would shift these costs off to taxes, would benefit both monopoly capital and monopoly labor unions, while increasing the taxes on competitive domestic industries.

Therefore, it is in the interest of certain sectors of the bourgeoisie to cast about for solutions to growing working-class unrest, particularly in anticipation of the continued attack on the standard of living and working conditions of labor. Pernicious social-democratic reforms, such as the "Dellums Bill," have the virtue of appearing to provide desperately needed social services, which are being slashed due to rising costs and limited tax revenues. Social-democratic worker participation can head off righteous demands for workers' control, while guaranteeing labor peace and long-term planning of labor costs.

Thus, the "Dellums Bill" offers to the profiteering health industry a "reasonable" answer consonant with capitalism, to the militant actions of health workers demanding decent wages, humane social services and control over their labor processes. It provides for collusion of workers in their own exploitation and sets up as their bosses the "community," not the state or the bourgeoisie. With boards of "community members" and "workers" supposedly representing their interests, how do workers take action? This bill would not provide "democratic reform" for the working class, but rather strengthen the hegemony of the bourgeoisie and petty bourgeoisie, bringing state neo-capitalism in the health industry to fuller bloom, and further curtailing avenues of struggle available to the proletariat and eliminating "labor unrest."

The Neighborhoods Decide Everything

Community control as called for in the "Dellums Bill," in a capitalist society is none other than bourgeois democracy: the rule of the privileged minority over the oppressed majority. Marx speaks to the inherent inequality of the bourgeois democratic process in Critique of the Gotha Programme when he attacks the bourgeois concept of equal rights for people who are in an unequal condition. Lenin spells it out further in State and Revolution:

> Every right is an application of an equal measure to different people who in fact are not alike, are not equal to one another; that is why "equal right" is really a violation of equality and an injustice...In capitalist society...democracy is always hemmed in by the narrow limits set by capitalist exploitation, and consequently always remains, in reality, a democracy for the minority, only for the propertied classes, only for the rich. (10)

What does Lenin mean by "hemmed in"? First, democracy only applies to a small sphere of the lives of the working class. On the job, where most of a worker's life is determined, there are no votes over what is produced, by whom, under what conditions, for what wages. And in the sphere in which "democracy" holds sway, only those with money to run for office and with control of the media have a fighting chance to take critical positions in the state apparatus. In addition, the rich consistently buy government officials with more campaign contributions, weekend junkets, job offers for government regulatory bureaucrats, and fancy lawyers to get the laws written and enforced as they wish. As Marx pointed out, "the oppressed are allowed once every few years to decide which particular representatives of the oppressing class should represent and suppress them in parliament." (11) While the writers of the "Dellums Bill" would no doubt agree on the above, they persist in proclaiming the same old bourgeois democratic procedures for our health system. Why don't these social democrats understand that elections for community health boards will equally come under the control of those with political and economic power?

"But wait," the bill writers will say, "the health system is being constructed from the bottom up. The neighborhoods decide everything." Geographically, perhaps, it's from the bottom up. But in terms of classes, it's the same old "from the top down." Who in the neighborhood – especially the poor minority neighborhood – has the time and money to run for community board, the contacts with the media and the community institutions to get out their vote, the education to articulate their ideas in this verbally oriented society? It's the small real estate man down the block, not the woman who takes care of his kids; it's the social worker, not the welfare mother; it's the respected minister of the neighborhood church, not the unemployed clerical worker. In short, it's the petty bourgeoisie, not the working class, that will get control of community health boards.

And it's not just the elected board members who will wield control of the health institutions. It's also the university-trained administrator with the expertise and jargonese to twist board members around his little finger: the "medical advisory board" which will self-servingly advise the board, in the "best interest of the patients," of course, and the board lawyer who has the mystified knowledge to interpret this very "Dellums Bill" and thereby cow the board members into unquestioningly accepting his advice. Again, it's the petty bourgeoisie, elected or not elected, which will run the neighborhood based health system.

For those who still don't see the inevitability of petty bourgeois control over community health boards, let's look at our experience with demands for community participation and control in the 1960's.

A study of over 130 Community Action Projects in 63 cities revealed that the people receiving the services did not have any significant power, and that the projects were controlled by "middle class elements." (12) Most Model Cities programs involved community groups dominated by the "upwardly mobile" and not by real representatives of the masses of people in the neighborhoods. In most situations, the professional staff made the decisions. (13) Dr. Jack Geiger, one of the first people involved with community control of health services in the 1960's, points out that most often selection of community board members "does not involve the great majority of the community's population in any way. (Board members are)...almost always the existing elite in the community...who have strong political or ideological motivations." (14) An analysis by Health/PAC New York's North East Neighborhoods Association (NENA) Health Center quotes Ms. Bertha Dixon, co-chair of the NENA health committee: "The problem with community-wide elections is that the same old politicos who have organized their faction get elected." Health/Pac adds, "Once on the committee, verbal skills and endurance limit effective participation even further," concluding that white, basically "middle class" people are the most prominent on the health committee. (15) At Mission Neighborhood Health Center in San Francisco, a successful community fight to dislodge a professionally-dominated board led to a new board controlled by a psychologist, a university instructor, a minister and several other petty bourgeois people. The working-class patients on the board, who spoke only Spanish, were of such minor consequence that when board meetings really became heated and got to the heart of a matter, the Spanish translations were overlooked. In short:

> Small political subdivisions tend to place power in the hands of a few who tyrannize the many....When the attention of the poor is taken from basic social injustice and riveted on issues of community control, important and fundamental social change is avoided....If one subscribed to a conspiratorial view of American society, one might well imagine the most powerful figures in the military-industrial complex designing an anti-poverty program whereby poor people who do not participate in standard political processes would be diverted to toy elections and to fighting among themselves over the control of pitifully inadequate sums of money. (16)

Doctors and Clerks – "Workers" All

Within its idealistic framework, the "Dellums Bill" calls for worker control of health facilities. First, the law provides that it is up to each area board to ensure the democratic control by the workers. As we have already shown, because of the petty bourgeois character of these community boards, they can hardly be counted upon to take a stand for workers over whom they are responsible. In fact, the experience of "community controlled" neighborhood health centers has borne out time and again that the "community" board will, more often than not, come down against the workers. At San Francisco General Hospital, the Community Board of the outpatient department instituted time clocks in order to discipline the community health workers and clerical staff. Often pressures from federal and private granting agencies have forced them to even harsher disciplinary measures as a test of their ability to administer their grant.

Secondly, the "Dellums Bill" piously speaks of ending the domination of professionals in health care. The bill would in fact institutionalize, under the guise of "workers' control," the hegemony of the professionals and administrators (the petty bourgeoisie). According to the bill, a "worker" is defined as anyone employed by the National Community Health Service, including those who provide services (including doctors), teach, administer or do research. If anything, this would increase the administrators and technocrats vying for control with the doctors and nurses, all using the working class as their base of legitimacy and their own "employee" status as their right to continue as bosses.

This has been borne out in the experience at one clinic in San Francisco. When the clinic opened, a steering committee was established to represent the views of all "workers" in the matters of the clinic. Over its first year of existence, the steering committee was demoted to an "advisory" role to the director. It had no role in such affairs as layoffs and budget allocations, but was consulted about redecorations of the clinic and staff parties. The committee was composed of one representative for each employment category: faculty, residents, administration, nurses, social work, clerical and family health workers. In practice, that meant a meeting of three doctors, one administrator, one registered nurse, one social worker – all petty bourgeois – and two workers.

Under the guise of "one big happy family," many new programs were developed for better patient care – behavioral science, preventive medicine, prenatal counseling. All the while the clinic's budget and staff were being slashed. Workloads were sped up, clerical staff cut in half; but the workers were told to keep at it, since "we all are working for the patients." Of course, the administrators' and doctors' reputations grew off their innovative programs (with all the more wonderment, pulling off such programs in the midst of a budget crisis). The R.N.'s and social workers enjoyed teaching classes and counseling, rather than the drudgery of temperatures and welfare forms. These tasks were left to L.V.N.'s, orderlies and family health workers. But as the staff turnover rose and the waiting time for patients lengthened, the myth of worker participation wore thin. Disciplinary measures tightened and it became clear to all involved that the underlying management techniques were no different than in any traditional clinic.

As the clinic example illustrates, social-democratic reformism results in the continued domination and exploitation of the worker, the critical distinction between petty bourgeois and proletarian socialism. The "Dellums Bill" attaches a veneer of worker participation onto the basic capitalist labor process and then sets as one of its objectives "efficient and accountable operation and management." One might ask, "Efficiency and accountability – aren't those goals in a socialist society as well?" Given the domination by petty bourgeois technocrats and managers prescribed in the "Dellums Bill," we understand this call for accountability as accountability to the petty bourgeoisie, this call for efficiency as efficiency gained at the expense of the workers, as modern management achieved by the most advanced methods designed and tested under capitalism, that is, Taylorism or scientific management.

Efficiency in Health Care:
A Scientific Approach

Scientific management was introduced into industrial production by Frederick Taylor in the last decades of the 19th century, as a method for asserting the absolute control of management over the labor process. Taylor realized that the individual craftsman's knowledge of a skill allowed him freedom and judgement in his work, as well as the ability to withhold that knowledge to resist speedup and disciplinary control. Taylorism sought to break down the division of labor by skill and replace it with division of labor by detail, wherein each individual worker knows only a tiny aspect of the whole and has each facet prescribed exactly by management. As Harry Braverman points out in Labor and Monopoly Capital:

> Modern management('s)...role was to render conscious and systematic, the formerly unconscious tendency of capitalist production. It was to ensure that as a craft declined, the worker would sink to the level of general and undifferentiated labor

power, adaptable to a large range of simple tasks, while as science grew, it would be concentrated in the hands of management. (17)

Within the capitalist economy, scientific management is a primary tool for gaining an efficient and disciplined labor force. And the "Dellums Bill" would seek to perpetuate these methods. By calling for "more efficient use of allied workers," the "Dellums Bill" would result in more and more detail workers. Yes – under the guise of job enrichment, orderlies can be trained to do many different functions. This in fact is occurring as capitalist investment and its consequent Taylorist methods of management further invade the health industry. This cheapens the labor costs, by employing more workers of lower skill and educational training, and increases management's control over the workforce, as each worker has less knowledge of the patient's total needs. As we analyze the changes in the labor process occurring in health care today, we do not think this results in better care for patients.

The fact that no attention is paid to the labor process of health care derives from the petty bourgeois character of the Dellums conception. We find it no accident that petty bourgeois intellectuals and professionals cannot conceive of changing the process in which health care is delivered. Most petty bourgeois people basically like what they do: doctors by and large enjoy taking care of patients, researchers enjoy doing their research. It is usually when their ability to do what they like to do becomes limited that the petty bourgeois professionals begin to feel oppressed and become radicalized. Therefore, the petty bourgeoisie conceives of reforms which benefit its own working conditions, while asserting the pious homily that reforms in its working conditions will also benefit the mass of labor beneath it. But a petty bourgeois utopia always includes the vision that the working class should remain the working class – perhaps utilized a bit more efficiently, with a bit more comfort on their jobs.

The petty bourgeoisie cannot conceive of the elimination of the working class as a class, for its existence forms the basis for petty bourgeois class distinction. Out of their own fear of falling back into the proletariat, the petty bourgeoisie conceive only of individuals escaping from the class. The petty bourgeois socialist answer to this dilemma is to offer to a chosen few from the working class, the reward of advancement to the petty bourgeoisie. Thus the emphasis in the "Dellums Bill" is placed on advancement up the career ladder, not changing the basic labor process for the entire working class.

Many of the concrete proposals on employee relations are regressive acts towards hospital workers, who have been among the militant sectors of the labor force. Collaboration between labor and management is elaborated through collective bargaining and civil service acts, which maintain the inequities of salary based on skills, education and experience. Nowhere does the bill provide for limitations on salaries of physicians and other professionals. The right-to-strike, which only in recent years has become an active tool for hospital workers, is limited by the bill, according to the deemed wishes of the community board. The NCHS workers are designated as federal employees, whose legal access to the right-to-strike has been consistently abrogated by cries of the "public's right to government services." The effect of these provisions would be to emasculate and legalize the burgeoning militancy among health workers. Finally, the class collaboration intended by the bill becomes crystal clear. The Dellumites hope to "encourage cooperation and mutual respect" among employees, which we can only interpret as hoping to blur over the class interests of the working class and petty bourgeoisie, dampen class struggle within the health arena and reinforce the hegemony of the petty bourgeoisie.

The Dellums proponents protest: "That is not our intent – we want to make the health system better." Better for whom? We must conclude – for the petty bourgeoisie. Not only does the petty bourgeoisie claim control of the neighborhood boards and the administration of the health facilities. The "Dellums Bill" promotes the petty bourgeoisie as a class by providing many more jobs for petty bourgeois professionals, technocrats and administrators in their welfare state bureaucracy. For the minority of doctors who would not be opposing "big government" interference in their traditional petty bourgeois entrepreneurship, such a federal system would guarantee a comfortable salary, a free office and no hassle about malpractice insurance. The career hopes of health planners and community service agency administrators could run rampant, offering possibilities unmet by OEO, HEW, CHP, HSA, ad nauseum.

The Health of Working People

Our next major concern is how the health of the working class will fare under the "Dellums Bill." Any public health person knows that the health of lower income people is markedly worse than the health of the wealthy:

> Over the years, studies have shown a higher rate of sickness in the lower social classes, whether "class" was ranked by measurement of income level...or by educational attainment or occupational status or by combinations of these factors. (18)

Although the U.S. government does not put its statistics in class terms, the reality is impossible to hide.

—30% of all people with yearly income less than $3,000 are disabled, yet only 8% with income over $10,000 are so afflicted. And these figures are not simply due to more elderly people falling in the low income category; the health differences hold within each age group.

—In the age group 45-64, half of the people with family income less than $3,000 are disabled but only 13% with income more than $15,000 are disabled.

—People with family income less than $5,000 suffer 60% more restricted-activity days each year than the average person, 50% more days disabled in bed, and 60% more days in the hospital.

—Children whose fathers are service workers or laborers show a 50% greater infant mortality rate than those of professionals and managers.

—For many specific diseases such as hypertension, heart disease, bronchitis and diabetes, people of lower incomes have higher morbidity and mortality rates than those with higher incomes. (19)

Although the first purpose of the "Dellums Bill" is to make available "health care services which emphasize the enhancement and maintenance of health as well as the treatment of illness," there is nothing in the bill which addresses the major causes of illness and eliminates those causes. For, in fact, to eliminate those causes requires the overthrow of the economic system rather than the passage of a comprehensive health service.

The drafters of the bill will cry, "We never intended to solve all the problems. We just wanted to improve health care and raise consciousness. We know this health service can't prevent the illnesses of the working class."

If they wish to raise consciousness, why do they pretend

to "emphasize the enhancement and maintenance of health" when they know full well the bill doesn't do that? If anything, such a promise lowers consciousness since it isn't true. And in terms of improving health care, we doubt that very much – given who will still be running the state if the Dellums advocates have their way.

Ample evidence of the petty bourgeois class nature of the "Dellums Bill" also comes from the listing of basic health rights. The rights are by and large geared to the well-educated consumer who wants a broad choice of possibilities and an outpouring of information. Very few of the rights have real meaning for the working class. For one promise of transportation, childcare and homemaking services to ensure access to helath services, the bill lists over 20 detailed rights concerned with receipt of information and choices of treatment – choices more concerned with petty bourgeois self-indulgence than with ensuring a high technical quality of care. So long as the individual is made to "feel" well, it is not so important whether the actual conditions of health are improved, whether a person actually gets better.

People have the right to a comprehensive dictionary of terms in health services, but there is no right to health services on nights and weekends so that working people can get cared for without losing a day's pay or a job. Pregnant women have the right to delivery at home, but no right to decent food during pregnancy that would truly increase the chances of a healthy child. While people have the right to "dignity" while receiving health services, never are working people guaranteed a job that doesn't clog up their lungs with dusts which lead them to a slow, agonizing, breathless death.

Not that most of the promised rights can in practice be guaranteed. But if the rights are any indicator of the class concerns of this health service, it is a service more for the professor than for the waitress, more for the engineer than for the coal miner.

The Petty Bourgeoisie Reaps the Benefits

The futility of reformism in health care as manifested in the United States must be seen in terms of whom these reforms have most benefited. Amid great controversy, in 1965 Medicare and Medicaid legislation was enacted. It soon became apparent that it was the bourgeoisie, in the form of multinational drug companies, insurance companies and medical equipment and supply companies that reaped the greatest harvest of the federal financing of health care for the poor and elderly. Also abundantly filling their coffers were members of the petty bourgeoisie, mainly professionals, adminstrators, salaried managers, bureaucrats, and technocrats, who were guaranteed payment for care of the poor and elderly – financed by a tax base which proportionately hit the working class the hardest. Petty bourgeois salaries have, for the most part, climbed steadily. More importantly, their ability to control the work of others has increased dramatically over the past decades. These administrators and professionals, as class representatives of the petty bourgeoisie, uphold the class interests of this subsector of society.

The technocrats of the petty bourgeoisie firmly believe that it is only the "experts" who can solve the people's problems. Furthermore, they see themselves as members of the "new working class" by virtue of the fact that they possess no economic or occupational independence and are employed by capital. By seeing its interests and working class interests as the same, this new petty bourgeoisie eliminates itself as a class, disguises the class contradictions between itself and the working class, and with its expertise can establish petty bourgeois hegemony over the proletariat in the name of the proletariat. Its solutions include more technocracy, more administration and more paternalism and benevolence towards health workers and patients. This is the essence of the "Dellums Bill."

There is a contradictory character to the new petty bourgeoisie, for it takes its characteristics from both the bourgeoisie and the proletariat. As part of the capital accumulation process, it receives some of the rewards of capital. But as employees who occupy a subordinate position, petty bourgeois individuals begin to experience the pressures of the proletarian condition. Thus they feel pressured from all sides. With rising inflation, increasing unemployment and massive social service cutbacks, the privileges they enjoy begin to be eroded, and with this come the fear and insecurities the working class experiences daily.

These contradictions weigh heavily on them, forcing them to seek reformist solutions, all the while realizing that the only way they can increase their power is through the power of the working class. Indeed, the only hope of the petty bourgeoisie is the working class. Therefore, the petty bourgeoisie moves in its own interest towards social-democratic, electoral reform. This again is what the "Dellums Bill" represents. It epitomizes welfare state capitalism, where the basic relations of capitalism remain, including that of the capitalist labor process. This is petty bourgeois socialism, in which the petty bourgeoisie increases and stabilizes its share of the national income while only minimally improving the economic conditions of the working class so as to pacify it. Social democracy or petty bourgeois socialism, as embodied in the "Dellums Bill," must not be confused with a genuinely revolutionary position.

Proletarian socialism calls for a new society where the relations of production are altered such that petty bourgeois and bourgeois hegemony is no longer possible. This cannot be done through piecemeal cooptable reforms, but only through the transformation of society in which private property, the capitalist labor process and exploitation are abolished. In their places must come collective ownership of the means of production and new and human labor processes through which human potential can be fully realized in a collectivity. The health of our people, as individuals and as a collectivity, depends ultimately on the health of our society. Only when the interests of the society reflect the interests, aspirations and goals of the majority of people – the working class – will we realize our full potential as creative and humane beings.

NOTES

1. Andre Gorz, "Workers' Control is More Than Just That," Workers' Control, ed. G. Hunnius et al. (New York, Vintage Press, 1973), p. 326.
2. Ibid., p. 326.
3. Ibid., p. 329.
4. German Trade Union Federation, "Co-determination in the Federal Republic of Germany," Workers' Control, p. 196.
5. Helmut Schauer, "Critique of Co-determination," Workers' Control, pp. 215-16.
6. Ibid., p. 221.
7. Lars Karlsson, "Industrial Democracy in Sweden," Workers' Control, pp. 188-89.
8. Ibid., p. 184.
9. Andre Gorz, Strategy for Labor (Boston, Beacon Press), p. 12.

10. V.I. Lenin, State and Revolution (Peking, Foreign Languages Publishing House, 1973), pp. 103-10.
11. Karl Marx, Critique of the Gotha Programme (New York, International Publishers, 1966), p. 9.
12. Naomi Levine, "Community Participation: Some Hard Lessons," Congress Biweekly, December 19, 1969, pp. 3-7.
13. Sherry Arnstein, "A Ladder of Citizen Participation," AIP Journal (July, 1969).
14. H. Jack Geiger, "Community Control or Community Conflict?", National TB and Respiratory Disease Association Bulletin (November, 1969), pp. 4-10.
15. Health/PAC Bulletin (June 1972).
16. Bertram M. Beck, "Community Control: A Distraction, Not an Answer," Social Work (October, 1969).
17. Harry Braverman, Labor and Monopoly Capital (New York, Monthly Review Press, 1974), pp. 120-21.
18. Milton Roemer, et al., "Health Insurance Effects," Ann Arbor School of Public Health (University of Michigan, 1972), p. 35.
19. U.S. Department of Health, Education and Welfare, Health, U.S. 1975, HEW Publication #(HRA) 76-1232.

When Work is Soulless,
Life Stifles and Dies

Labor Process and Health

Andrew Coren M.D.

Without work all life goes rotten.
But when work is soulless, life
stifles and dies. (Camus)

The industrialization of the American health care system
has brought with it, over the past 15 years, an increasing
application of socio-economics to the health sciences.
Bourgeois institutions have blossomed with research: whole
departments are devoted to health planning, social and
community medicine, epidemiologic research and preventive
medicine. These developments, arising in part from the
demands of health professionals and health activists, have
served only the needs of capitalism. In the late sixties petty
bourgeois health activists protested against the inequities of
the health care system, against workplace disease, against
racism, sexism and poverty in this country and atrocities in
Vietnam. They demanded health care as a right, calling out

to society to look at the costly destruction of human life within the capitalist system. And capitalism responded by developing a technology to analyze the "cost problem" and cut the costs to capitalists, while maximizing profits from the health industry and increasing the misery of the working class.

Prevention has been one current focus of the health activist movement, covering a broad range of technology including community sanitation, environmental control, occupational health and safety, food, drug and now medical device controls, well baby care and family planning clinics, immunization programs and health education. Seeking to unite with working class forces, many petty bourgeois activists have concentrated heavily in the area of occupational safety and health, demanding in one form or another, more prevention. Never have these activists seriously analyzed what prevention is or whom it serves. Bourgeois technology, the product of capitalist relations of production and that which reproduces these relations, is accepted as given.

Prevention is designed to intervene in the relation between the worker and the physical, chemical and "emotional" hazards. The hazards are assumed. Such an environment makes prevention a commodity, to be bought and sold like any other commodity. The labor process and the division of labor in detail go unchallenged in the dealings over prevention and occupational safety and health. It is the organization of work which places the worker in contact with all of the hazards. This is no less true today than when Marx commented on it:

> Every organ of sense is injured in an equal degree by artificial elevation of the temperature, by dust-laden atmosphere, by the deafening noise, not to mention danger to life and limb among the thickly crowded machinery, which, with the regularity of the seasons, issues its list of the killed and wounded in the industrial battle. (1)

Bourgeois hazard prevention would never consider slow-down or fewer hours of work (with increased employment) to reduce the intensity of noise, concentration of dust and fumes in the air, and total dose of exposure to safe levels. The needs of capitalism for unemployment, ever longer hours, and more intensified work would not permit that solution. Instead, protective devices, such as breathing

46

machines and masks, ear muffs, and various filtering and baffling systems, are produced (with equal hazards in this industry) and sold at a handsome profit!!

For many petty bourgeois professionals and activists, the organization of work characteristic of capitalism and the consequent social relations it produces go unquestioned as necessities of modern industrial society. This ideology holds technology as the determinant condition of the social relations of production, rather than the other way around. Consequently, this ideology holds that there will be division of labor in detail as long as there is modern industry. This technological determinism denies the dialectical materialist relations between technology, labor process and capitalist relations, and is itself a form of bourgeois ideology. The demands of the petty bourgeois health movement, dependent upon the capitalist relations of production, accept and promote the bourgeois ideology which presumes that things must always stay as they are.

Casualties on the Job

The labor process and technology are not, in fact, givens. They are developed and implemented totally in the service of capital, to be used as weapons by capital against labor. It is no wonder that we see casualties from the labor process — human suffering and death:

   −In 1968, over 14,000 Americans were killed in industrial accidents, about the same as the number killed in Vietnam. In the same year, 90,000 workers suffered permanent disability and 2.1 million suffered temporary disability from industrial accidents. Industrial disease strikes between 400,000 and 25 million workers and kills between 4,000 and 100,000 American workers each year, by conservative estimates.
   −Occupational factors may very well play a far more significant role than is presently realized in the causation of the major diseases and health problems that confront us.
   −Cancer and heart disease are the two leading causes of death in America. Environmental factors may account for 90% of the cancer in this country. The large increase in the prevalence of heart disease recorded in recent years appears to be closely related to our "changing occupational profile." (2)

This outrageous balance sheet only scratches the surface of the totality of human destruction wrought by the capitalist labor process. The classic Marxian conception of the relation between the conscious activity of human beings and their labor reveals the very species character which is violated by the capitalist labor process.

Conception, the ability to construct an image in the human mind before creating it in reality, is the facility which allows man to transcend the productive capabilities of all other animals, not only quantitatively but qualitatively. The human mind can conceive of the object of creation, as well as the methods, tools and materials by which it should be created. Thus, mankind is not limited by instinct in what it can make or the manner in which it can be made. Because man can conceptualize, he can also take himself, the species and the whole world as the object of his labors. It is conscious activity which makes humans truly free. They are free from an isolated existence, since self-consciousness allows them to conceive of themselves as part of the world, as members of a species of conscious beings, enabling them to create, according to this conception, a social world. Truly human labor is not merely a means of existence but is a means of changing the whole nature of existence and life itself.

The capitalist labor process reverses this activity, turns the freedom of creative and social production of the species into a prison for the laborer in which every product made is expropriated by the capitalist and used to further imprison the species. Every act of production is strictly prescribed and controlled by the capitalist. The division of labor in detail is imposed to achieve capitalist control over the laboring class, with the intent of destroying the human species character by dividing conception from execution.

> To subdivide a man is to execute him if he deserves the sentence, to assassinate him if he does not....The subdivision of labor is the assassination of a people. (3)

The division of labor in detail is the disease which most afflicts mankind, an epidemic which affects the working class in every industry, including the health industry. It is unique to capitalism and is not a necessity of modern industry. As the basic method by which capital enslaves labor, division of labor in detail is a necessity of capitalism and work cannot be reorganized without it. Nor can capitalism be overthrown without attacking the labor process which daily creates the conditions for dominance of one class over another.

This analysis escapes most petty bourgeois professionals and activists. "We can at least prevent the immediate causes of discomfort," say petty bourgeois reformers. They are affected by the atomization of their own work so that even they do not see the overview or the effect of their work on the whole. Yet, as technocrats, managers, engineers, doctors, social workers and registered nurses, their share in control provides them with a stake in the system of control. Therefore it does not serve them to attack the labor process which is also their method of control. Reforms like prevention are in their class interest, providing this stratum with more jobs, more prestige, more power and security. Petty bourgeois socialism would preserve their hegemony over the technology and turn state power over to these technocrats.

The proletariat, however, cannot help but be conscious of the effects of the labor process. That consciousness is given expression in the resistance of the labor force:

> Dull, repetitive, seemingly meaningless tasks offering little autonomy are causing discontent at all occupational levels. (4)
> The productivity of the worker is low — as measured in absenteeism, turnover rates, wildcat strikes, sabotage, poor quality products, and a reluctance by workers to commit themselves to their work tasks. Moreover, a growing body of research indicates that as work problems increase, there may be a consequent decline in physical health and mental health, family stability, community participation and cohesiveness, and balanced sociopolitical attitudes. (Emphasis added) (5)

As one welder put it:

> A job should be a job, not a death sentence...the whole thing was: Damn it, it's about time we took a stand....We stopped the line (he pauses and grins). (6)

Resistance by labor is not a new phenomenon: it existed from the beginning of the division of labor in the manufacturing period, prior to the age of the scientific-technological revolution and even prior to the industrial revolution:

> ...throughout the whole manufacturing period there runs the complaint of want of discipline among the workmen. (7)

"Want of discipline" – resistance – has lately reached such incredible proportions that the bourgeoisie has taken more notice. A report in Fortune magazine notes that in 1970 absenteeism in auto plants averaged 5%, rising to 10% on Fridays; tardiness increased making it more difficult to start up production lines; quit rates ranged from 25% to 30% per year. In 1969 at the Ford assembly plant in Wixom, Michigan, the quit rate was 7% each month. White collar and service industries show the same phenomena with 30% annual turnover rates. (8)

Scientific Management for the Health Industry

Resistance among service workers has paralleled the economic growth of the service industries, and consequent introduction of technology, cost control and labor discipline mechanisms in these fields. A clear example can be found in the health industry, where the de-skilling of the labor force has been intimately and dialectically tied to the flow of capital.

Production of the commodity health services is, like other commodities, dependent upon market variables. Between 1965-1974 total national expenditures for health and medical services increased by about 270%. Largely due to Medicaid/Medicare, federal expenditures in this area increased by about 390% during the same period. Because of the lack of controls on the federal dollars, which were systematically being ripped off by professionals and institutions alike, health care prices quickly inflated, making the health industry tremendously profitable. This attracted large amounts of private capital which went, directly or indirectly, toward the development of increased technology in the health care industry. The technologies included those necessary for hospital construction, the new marketing technology of health planning (medical care distribution: Health Maintenance Organizations, Regional Medical Programs, etc.) and the application of traditional management technologies to the health industry.

Inflation within the medical care industry, however, contributes to the overall inflationary pressure on the cost-of-living index and hence to labor costs of production for the capitalists. Therefore, the federal goverment has spear-headed a general "belt tightening" in the health industry, leading to shutdowns of hospitals right and left. Health planning has been used to insure maximal utilization of the remaining facilities, while tens of thousands of health care workers (primarily working class) are joining the unemployed, and their employed counterparts are being tremendously sped up. New technology in hospital construction has "rationalized" transportation (with pneumatic tubes and better layout), communications (centrex telephones and other centralized personnel call systems) and patient observation (with television monitoring and other centralized monitoring devices). It has centralized specialty medical wards (e.g. critical care), auxiliary medical services (e.g. respiratory therapy) and hospital support services (e.g. central supply). These measures have removed more and more workers from the essential responsibility of observing and caring for patients, making them machine operators instead of people taking care of people.

With the effective implementation of modern scientific management techniques for the workers, the initial objections of doctors and other petty bourgeois professionals have been replaced by a willing cooperation. An example of this is taken from "Trends Affecting the U.S. Health Care System," a report to the Department of Health, Education, and Welfare:

> With the growing role of administrators has come the growing use of electronic equipment to schedule hospital admissions, analyze the results of laboratory tests, keep medical records, and check differences in physicians' patterns of care. Tele-monitoring of patients has become a valuable aid in the hospital. Multiphasic screening is employing automated testing machines, which enable para-medical personnel to run patients through batteries of tests more quickly and at less cost than ever before. (9)

A report sponsored by the Office of Research and Development, Manpower Administration, U.S. Department of Labor (1975) presents a guide to the implementation of scientific management techniques in hospitals, subdividing the labor force into detail workers:

> The committee must adopt a job description and list of important functions for each major health care

occupation....more sophisticated functions will be performed by the higher-rated occupations, and the less sophisticated or simpler tasks will be performed by the lower-rated occupations...the restructuring committee should take a long look at the current hiring-in requirements. For example, is it necessary for aides or ward clerks to have high school diplomas? (10)

Similar guidelines were developed and applied in general industry at the turn of the century. Frederick Winslow Taylor, the father of scientific management and the originator of time and motion studies, established three basic principles. His first:

The managers assume...the burden of gathering together all of the traditional knowledge which in the past has been possessed by the workmen and then of classifying, tabulating, and reducing this knowledge to rules, laws and formulae....(11)

This dissociation of the labor process from the skills of the workers sets the foundation for complete management control. For the health industry, this process is moving ahead at full force.

Taylor's predecessor in management technology, Charles Babbage, explained why such labor practices were profitable to capital:

The master manufacturer, by dividing the work to be executed into different processes, each requiring different degrees of skill or of force, can purchase exactly that precise quantity of both which is necessary for each process, whereas if the whole work were to be executed by one workman, that person must possess sufficient skill to perform the most difficult, and sufficient strength to execute the most laborious of the operations into which the article is divided. (12)

Under capitalism, "The one-sidedness and deficiencies of the detail laborer become perfections when he is part of the collective labor process." (13) It is objectively untrue that skill and knowledge are more important in an age of industry and high technology. Capitalists, through restructuring the labor process, are consciously selecting for untrained individuals. Results: one registered nurse is utilized to supervise many licensed vocational nurses and nurse's aides who clean patients, make beds, take vital signs, pass out medicines, sometimes change wound dressings, etc. One social worker now supervises several health workers (mainly welfare mothers paid 1/3 the salary) who learn the socio-economic problems of the patients and their families, make referrals to community agencies, and often make home visits to assess patients' medical conditions – doing the work of the hospital L.V.N.

Taylor's second principle is that "all possible brainwork should be removed from the shop and centered in the planning or laying-out department...."(14) This is the final separation of conception from execution in productive labor. Planning in the health care industry is divided among the various professionals, specialists and management personnel. More and more workers are being habituated to performing tasks. The task method is Taylor's third principle, by which the work process is implemented without giving to the worker an ounce of knowledge, overview, input or control.

Long thought to be resistant to the application of principles of scientific management, the service industries are increasingly subject to it. Speed-ups and intensification of work are being instituted in hospitals and clinics across the country. Under the influence of the funding from the Department of Health, Education, and Welfare and the regulations and market demands that came with it, public hospitals' admission rates are increasing while the length of stay in the hospitals is driven down – leading in part to the overbedding crisis. At the same time, workers are being laid off, resulting in more hurried care, fewer services and increasing resistance by the workers to the labor process. With an increase in yearly hospital-worker injuries and an increase in "newly discovered" job-related disease in the health industry, work itself in the health industry may someday be classified as a major "iatrogenic" industrial disease.

Job Safety – A Capitalist View

The crisis of world capitalism has forced the U.S. out of its former position of unquestioned economic hegemony, placing stringent limits on budget deficits. Thus the problems of the inflated cost of medical care have forced the bourgeoisie to look for alternatives:

> Job safety became a matter of self-interest to both management and labor when reducing accidents on the job could reduce insurance premiums. (15)

In addition, the capitalists have begun to look at the costs they are bearing as a result of the capitalist labor process:

> The total cost of occupational hazards was estimated by the National Safety Council at $9.3 billion during 1973 – nearly 1% of the GNP. This figure, moreover, is likely to be a gross understatement of even the direct costs to the GNP of both occupational injuries and illnesses. An estimated 25 million workdays were lost through absenteeism during 1972...a loss of 100,000 man years of work.

Nor has the bourgeoisie failed to examine the level of resistance to the work process and the possible risk of social unrest:

> There is now convincing evidence that some blue-collar workers are carrying their work frustrations home and displacing them in extremist social and political movements or hostility toward the government. (17)

The response of the capitalists, now as before, is not reform but the further control and exploitation of the working class. For capital accepts as "natural" the antagonisms of the workplace:

> Fundamentally, the basic conflict of self-interests stems from managements' desires to keep costs down and to maintain control of the workplace versus workers' desire to gain the largest possible package of wages, benefits, job security and control. (18)

Prevention must be seen as a form of technology enlisted in the service of capital, not for palliation of the workforce but for increased exploitation of it. One of the hotter items in capital's bag of tricks is job redesign and profit sharing. In response to worker resistance to the division of labor into miniscule tasks, the labor process is being redesigned so that workers do their tasks in teams. To dispel any charge of manipulation, management will often add a small cut of profits to workers' wages. The benefit to capital is clear:

> Using standard principles, industrial engineers had indicated that 110 workers would be needed...But when the team concept (rather than individual assignments) was applied...the result was a manning level of less than 70 workers....The major economic benefit has come from such factors as improved yields, minimized waste and avoidance of shutdowns. (19)

These technologies (prevention, pre-employment screening, industrial psychology, industrial relations, personnel administration, job redesign):

> ...do not by and large concern themselves with the organization of work, but rather with the conditions under which the worker may best be brought to cooperate in the scheme of work organized by the industrial engineer. (20)

Occupational health and safety is a revealing case in point. The purpose of capital invested in prevention is never for the benefit of the laborer. The driving forces of capital are accumulation (expropriation of the working class) and centralization (monopolization and expropriation of the smaller capitalists). The "safe workplace," called for by the petty bourgeois activists, will serve these same ends:

> The problems of industrial productivity...relate increasingly to occupational health and safety. (Therefore) On the management side, some industries are seeking a better understanding of the worker...to cope with the relative decrease in American industrial productivity – and this has brought about some increase in job safety and health consciousness. (21)

Occupational safety and health, utilized within the capitalist relations of production, is no philanthropic enterprise. It's dollars and cents to the capitalist – expropriation of the working class: "The evidence suggests that meeting the higher needs of workers can, perhaps, increase productivity from 5%-40%..."(22)

The economic impact of "prevention" on the competition between national economies and between members of the bourgeoisie is not overlooked either. A report from the National Commission on Materials Policy by the National Academies of Science and Engineering concludes:

> The meager empirical evidence available at this time suggests that the balance of payments, employment, and national income effects resulting from the domestic environmental controls are likely to be relatively small for the U.S....Thus a tentative conclusion is that the aggregate impact of domestic environmental controls should not be a matter of deep concern for policy makers. Of more importance are the short term impacts on particular firms and industries. (Emphasis added) (23)

This latter point is helpful in explaining why so many of the multinationals (DuPont for example) have pushed for O.S.H.A. legislation. Smaller corporations, which cannot afford the new technology with their limited capital, are put out of business, thereby assisting in the centralization of capital.

Lest there remain any question about the role of the state in controlling the application of the technology of prevention, the President's Report on Occupational Safety and Health clarifies this point: "Impact studies are, nonetheless, valuable safeguards against adopting standards that might otherwise result in unnecessarily high compliance costs to employers." (24)

In conclusion, prevention in today's economy is not what it appears to be. When one analyzes the material basis for disease, as well as the material basis and effects of the commodity "prevention," it becomes clear that demands for more prevention, "safe workplaces," even socialized medicine are not in the service of the working class. These demands, however, do serve the petty bourgeoisie by securing their class positions and establishing even more control over society by virtue of the hegemony of technocracy which the capitalist labor process guarantees them, whatever the mode of distribution. The technology of prevention has had little impact on the health of the working class, even on the diseases caused by the usual, recognized hazards. The most ubiquitous and profound threat to the species, the capitalist labor process, is never addressed by the technology of prevention or its petty bourgeois proponents. On the other hand, the assistance which this new "humane" technology may provide to the capitalist class in its exploitation and control of labor is being thoroughly and openly investigated – and looks very profitable indeed!

NOTES

1. Karl Marx, Capital, Vol. I (New York, International Publishers, 1967), pp. 425-26.
2. N.A. Ashford, Crisis in the Workplace (Cambridge, M.I.T. Press, 1975), p. 10.
3. D. Urquhart, quoted in Capital, Vol. I, p. 363.
4. Special Task Force to the U.S. Secretary of Health, Education, and Welfare, Work in America (Cambridge, M.I.T. Press, 1973), p. xv.
5. Ibid., p. xvi.
6. Phil Stallings, quoted in Studs Terkel, Working (New York, Avon Books, 1974), p. 226.
7. Capital, Vol. I, p. 367.
8. Judson Gooding, "Blue Collar Blues on the Assembly Line," Fortune (July 1970), p. 70.
9. Cambridge Research Institute, Trends Affecting the U.S. Health Care System (U.S. Dept. of Health, Education, and Welfare, No. HRA 76-14503, 1975), p. 32.
10. Office of Research and Development Manpower Administration, Guide to Restructuring Medical Manpower Occupations in Hospitals (U.S. Dept. of Labor, 1975), pp. 33-34.
11. Frederick Taylor, Principles of Scientific Management (New York, Norton Press, 1967), pp. 37-38.
12. Charles Babbage, quoted in Capital, Vol. I, p. 349.
13. Capital, Vol. I, p. 349.
14. Principles of Scientific Management, pp. 98-99.
15. Crisis in the Workplace, p. 19.
16. Ibid., p. 17.
17. Work in America, p. 30.
18. Crisis in the Workplace. p. 5.
19. Work in America, pp. 98-99.
20. Harry Braverman, Labor and Monopoly Capital (New York, Monthly Review Press, 1974), p. 140.
21. Crisis in the Workplace, p. 4.
22. Work in America, p. 30.
23. National Academies of Science and Engineering, "Report for the National Commission on Materials Policy," quoted in Crisis in the Workplace, p. 22.
24. President's Report on Occupational Safety and Health, (Washington, D.C., U.S. G.P.O., 1973), p. 14.

Mission Neighborhood Health Center:

A Case Study of the Department of Health, Education, and Welfare as a Counterinsurgency Agency

Thomas Bodenheimer M.D. and
Marlene Dixon

In the 1960's, working class communities all over the country, particularly minority inner city neighborhoods, exploded in violent anger. The federal government responded with a pacification or cooling-out program: the War on Poverty. The War on Poverty provided federal funds to bring a few programs into the community, to create a few jobs, and to buy off working class leaders who were a threat to those in power. In the course of this program of counterinsurgency, the War on Poverty took over a slogan of the 1960's, "community control," and turned it into its opposite; rather than control *by* the community, "community control" came to mean control *over* the working class majority of the community.

One of the War on Poverty's important programs was the neighbor-

This paper was first presented at the Society for the Study of Social Problems, August 1979.

hood health center program to provide ambulatory health care to low income people. This program, initially slated to reach 25 million people through 1,000 health centers, was scaled down to 125 centers serving only 1.5 million people. The standard view of the neighborhood health center program holds that its aims were 1) to bring high quality health care to people previously denied such care, 2) to provide employment opportunities and training to neighborhood residents, and 3) to allow community members to participate in the governance of the health centers (Davis and Schoen, 1978). A more realistic view sees the neighborhood health center program as a means to control, rather than to assist, minority working class populations. This paper takes the example of one neighborhood health center, Mission Neighborhood Health Center in San Francisco, to show how federal counterinsurgency works and to expose the class character of "community control."

The Exploitation of Patients at
Mission Neighborhood Health Center

Mission Neighborhood Health Center (MNHC) was opened in the late 1960's by the Office of Economic Opportunity, the War on Poverty's central agency, to provide health services to San Francisco's Mission District. More recently, MNHC has been funded by the federal Department of Health, Education, and Welfare (HEW), which took over many of the War on Poverty programs. MNHC is the only fully bilingual health service available to the tens of thousands of non-English speaking Latino people of San Francisco.

During its first years, MNHC was run by a medical entrepreneur who used MNHC funds to help develop his own private medical office building nearby (Hartman and Feshbach, 1974). In 1975, a months-long community struggle forced HEW to give the MNHC grant to the Mission Area Health Associates (MAHA), a new community group with a board of trustees whose majority was supposed to be elected by the health center's own patients. MAHA's victory was considered to be a triumph for community control at MNHC.

In 1977, a small clique of Latino youths gained control over the MAHA board of trustees. This clique ran a network of Mission District poverty agencies, mainly concerned with youth programs, including the Real Alternatives Program, Centro de Cambio and Mission Community Legal Defense. At MNHC they named another member of their clique to the $25,000 a year job as health center administrator, though their friend had no experience administering a health care institution.

By 1979 the health center was in shambles and its patients were up in arms. Patients were forced to wait in long lines to pay fees before being cared for. For several months, patients who had outstanding bills were not allowed to receive medical services until they settled their bills. Many patients were receiving incorrect bills for services they had never gotten or had already paid for. A number of competent health professionals and employees were terminated, sometimes leaving patients without their health care provider from one day to the next. The board had purchased an extremely expensive and poorly programmed computer that caused patients to wait an average of 1¾ hours to register at the health center. Transportation services for elderly patients were reduced while money was wasted on excess administrative salaries. The health center's financial deficit topped $200,000.*

Worst of all, the clique running the board refused to hold the yearly elections required by their own bylaws. As the *San Francisco Examiner's* columnist Guy Wright (1979a) put it,

> Board members whose terms expired more than a year ago still cling to their seats, adopting budgets, handing out raises, firing anyone who objects—and appointing friends to fill vacancies when anyone resigns from the board.

HEW, which has the responsibility of administering the MNHC grant, knew of and ignored or encouraged the mismanagement at the health center. HEW allowed the health center's administrative costs to increase from 21% to 28% of the budget (U.S. Department of HEW, 1979a), though HEW suggests that such costs not exceed 20%. HEW approved the purchase of the computer that was later investigated by the FBI for possible fraudulent bidding practices and kickbacks (U.S. Department of HEW, 1979b). HEW allowed the clinic's board members to continue in office beyond their legal terms of office without demanding immediate elections, and HEW repeatedly backed this board as the health center's legitimate governing body.

The Health Center's Patients Fight Back

In 1979, as a result of community pressure, new elections finally began. But in May, the clique controlling the board disqualified a

---

* Documentation for the facts presented in this paragraph come from numerous MNHC memos and from Dr. Bodenheimer's own experience of being employed at MNHC for 3 1/2 years before his firing in June 1979.

number of the candidates in the election. Board members and their supporters physically and verbally intimidated volunteers attempting to help get the election underway. A fight took place at the clinic between board members and volunteers, and the election never took place.

Thereupon, 70 patients of the health center sued the board and won a June 8 agreement that the elections must start immediately, under the supervision of a neutral third party. Still, no action was taken to hold the elections. With the help of the Rebel Worker Organization and the Grass Roots Alliance, worker and community organizations who had been asked to get involved, over 100 patients formed themselves into the Patients Defense Association. They arrived en masse at the June 20 MAHA board meeting to demand decisive patient representation in the running of the clinic. They were denied.

The Association, many of whose members were already refusing to use clinic services, voted to formally boycott the clinic. For four weeks, the patients picketed the clinic, marching, educating and persuading. Hundreds of patients honored the boycott, going without health care or using alternative health services set up by the Rebel Worker Organization. Patients sent hundreds of letters and petition signatures to their elected representatives in Washington. By the end of the boycott, the Patients Defense Association had grown to 800 members.

During the boycott, physical intimidation showed itself again. One Patients Defense Association activist had sugar poured into the gas tank of her car; another had her car windshield broken; and yet another had objects thrown at the windows of her home. Gangs of youths threateningly drove around the picket line, which was largely made up of women and children.

Finally, the Regional Health Administrator of HEW, Dr. Sheridan Weinstein, met with the Patients Defense Association and agreed to guarantee a fair election procedure. But at the same time that Dr. Weinstein was negotiating with the Association, his office was encouraging and financing a lawsuit against the very organizations (the Grass Roots Alliance, Rebel Worker Organization and the Institute for the Study of Labor and Economic Crisis) who were assisting the patients in their struggle for democratic elections and decent health care. This lawsuit, brought by the clique controlling the MAHA board, asked for $1 million in damages for libel and conspiracy.

HEW's promise to guarantee fair elections had little substance. The Patients Defense Association's lawyers were forced to go into court time and time again, and only after obtaining ten court orders did the elections finally take place. The MAHA board and its lawyers, using

HEW funds to finance one after another courtroom maneuver, delayed the elections in every way possible, including resisting a judge's order. HEW was clearly supporting the MAHA board and thereby keeping the organized working class patients from participating in the election. Only another massive letter writing appeal to government officials, combined with victory after victory in court, brought about the elections. On October 9, after an intense five-month struggle, the elections were concluded. All Patients Defense Association candidates won seats on the new MAHA board by overwhelming majorities.

HEW again moved to block organized working class power over the clinic. After reducing the clinic's budget, HEW laid down strict conditions to the new board requiring immediate crippling layoffs of clinic employees and cutbacks in services. Failure to meet these conditions would result in the replacement of the new MAHA board by another community agency. The new board, with its patient majority, is faced with running a clinic left in financial shambles by the old board and besieged by HEW cutbacks and threats to take the grant away. As columnist Guy Wright (1979b) put it,

> HEW, which gave the old board extra money because it was doing such a poor job, has cut back on funding for the new board, which must clean up the mess.

Analysis: HEW as Counterinsurgency

Historically, the federal government has spent money for welfare and social service programs only at times of mass insurgency by the working class (Piven and Cloward, 1971). In the 1930's, the government enacted social security, unemployment and welfare programs in response to the demonstrations and protests of millions of people, many organized by the growing Communist Party. The 1950's, with little organized working class unrest, produced almost no new social programs. But the 1960's, with its civil rights movement and urban rebellions, brought a massive increase in welfare expenditures; new health programs including Medicare, Medicaid and neighborhood health centers; educational programs such as Headstart; and "community action" and legal services programs to put some pressure on local and state governments. In fact, many of the War on Poverty programs were targeted into areas of actual or potential urban rebellion.

These federal moneys, then, served as a massive domestic counterinsurgency effort, designed to stop any effective working class protest that could take root and threaten the stability of the existing capitalist order. Domestic counterinsurgency works by 1) channeling money to programs which minimally alleviate the worst horrors of life in minority working class communities but which principally provide charity and create dependency on government funds, and 2) funneling the money through agencies that hire working class leaders and buy them off with $20,000 a year positions and with control over other jobs in the community. Those who would not be bought off in this manner were frequently assassinated or imprisoned, for example, leaders of the Black Panthers. Those who were coopted became known to many as poverty pimps, and formed a new stratum of society, a stratum created by the needs of the state to control the working class in minority neighborhoods (*Rebel Worker News Journal*, 1979). The poverty pimps became the managers of the counterinsurgency programs, and as such gained control over aspects of the lives of the working class majority in their communities. Their control was termed "community control" because the poverty pimps came from the community. In this sense, "community control" has come to mean control *over* the working class community. The clique that ran the MAHA board from 1977 to 1979 is a clear example of this stratum of poverty pimps.

The Poverty Pimps: A Lumpen Petty Bourgeoisie

Using the terminology of Marxist class analysis, the poverty pimps are a new stratum of the lower rungs of the bourgeois class. Our society is made up of two antagonistic classes, the bourgeoisie (capitalist class) and the proletariat (working class) (Dixon, 1979). The capitalist class owns and controls the vast majority of the wealth—the land, the factories, the oil and natural resources. The working class is forced to work for the capitalist class in order to survive, and those unable to work become dependent upon and controlled by government programs such as social security, unemployment compensation, disability and such services as those offered by neighborhood health centers.

The lower strata of the bourgeois class are the petty (small) bourgeoisie, most of whom today are employed by capital or by the state as managers and professionals. Their function is to carry out the orders of the capitalists in controlling and commanding the day-to-day activities of the working class (Braverman, 1974). In the factory, this function is performed by the planners, managers and foremen; in the welfare system it is performed by the social workers. The petty bourgeoisie does not in itself possess control over the country's resources but, in return for financial rewards, it serves as a transmission belt of control between the bourgeoisie and the working class.

The stratum of the petty bourgeoisie that we call the poverty pimps is a new stratum, created by the counterinsurgency programs of the federal government. Their purpose is to manage these programs for the benefit of the government and thereby to pacify and control the working class on behalf of the bourgeoisie. Many poverty pimps may have taken their poverty agency positions with the best of intentions. But any desires to serve the community are snuffed out by the reality that they function as part of a state apparatus designed to rule and control their communities (*Rebel Worker News Journal*, 1979). The poverty pimps have a stake in maintaining the status quo in order to keep their own jobs. They may engage in petty (or big) ripoffs of public funds, and they create well-paying jobs for their friends and themselves to preserve and expand their positions and control. They come to identify with the government funding agency against their own people.

When the poverty funds begin to shrink, the poverty pimps may resort to any means—including using their own gangs—to keep their jobs and their control and to prevent themselves from being forced back into the working class whence they came. This stratum of poverty pimps is actually a *lumpen* petty bourgeoisie,* a stratum of parasites created by the War on Poverty, supported by taxpayers' money.

To conceal their true purpose from the working class that they exploit, those poverty pimps who are from minority communities may use the ideology of nationalism. For example,

> How can you criticize me, I'm Raza. We are united by the racism we experience, so you should support me. It doesn't matter that I make $30,000 a year while you and your family are on welfare. We are the same because my name is Gomez too (Martinez, 1979).

This kind of nationalism is a trick against the working class. It takes people's hatred of racism and twists it into a weapon against them (Martinez, 1979). And many white liberal and progressive people glorify the poverty pimps, calling them "The Community," when actually they are a tiny portion of the community that exploits the working class majority.

Domestic counterinsurgency and its creation of a lumpen petty bourgeoisie is in essence no different than the international counter-

---

* According to Marx, the *lumpen* proletariat are the petty criminals, pimps, small drug pushers—the poor who steal from the poor and exploit the poor, whose role in history is as a "bribed tool of reactionary intrigue."

insurgency which motivated such programs as the Alliance for Progress in the 1960's. The Alliance for Progress infused money into Latin America to pacify growing anti-American social movements.* It also created and strengthened a stratum of compradors (people who sold out the interests of their country for personal gain) similar to the poverty pimps, to administer the Alliance for Progress money and to control the population (for descriptions of world class formation, see Dixon, 1978; Jonas and Dixon, 1979). In its arsenal of counterinsurgency techniques, the Alliance for Progress utilized both the carrot and the stick: the food, agricultural and housing programs; and the repressive military and police apparatus.

HEW domestic counterinsurgency also utilizes both the carrot and the stick. The carrot is the charity of giving money to tranquilize the people and buy off their leaders; to make people depend on welfare checks, food stamps and neighborhood health centers; and thereby to prevent their organizing to really change their situation in society. The stick is to take away these charities if people cause trouble, a stick which is used to control both the poverty pimps and the working class. "Step out of line and you'll lose your little empire," the Feds tell the pimps. "Step out of line and you'll lose your food stamps, your clinics or your Headstart programs," the pimps tell the people (*Rebel Worker News Journal*, 1979).

Counterinsurgency at Mission Neighborhood Health Center

At MNHC, HEW counterinsurgency has shown itself as unwavering support for the poverty pimps, the small clique that controlled the MAHA board, against the organized working class patients. HEW knew for months that the board was violating its own bylaws by not holding elections, yet HEW continued to back them. In particular, when the Patients Defense Association, Rebel Worker Organization and Grass Roots Alliance began to work together to demand fair elections, HEW financed and encouraged the board's legal maneuvers to sabotage the elections and to sue the patients' supporters (Puga v. Hernandez, 1979). HEW attempted to discourage the patients and make them give up, and on several occasions blamed the patients for causing the problems at the

---

* The Alliance for Progress also served to create demand for U.S. products, which is an example of state capitalism – taxpayers' money funneled into corporate profits. HEW funding of health programs is also state capitalist as well as counterinsurgent, but that is not the subject of this paper.

clinic, problems for which HEW was actually responsible. And in encouraging the lawsuit against the patients' supporters, HEW was attempting to silence its own critics, showing no regard for freedom of speech and the right of responsible criticism.

The clique running the MAHA board acted in classic lumpen petty bourgeois fashion, with its financial exploitation of the working class — making the patients pay increased clinic fees (often in cash) to support the high administrative salaries voted by the board for their friends. The clique did everything in its power to keep the working class from taking away its control over the clinic. And the clique attempted to disorganize the patients by warning that further protest would cause HEW to close down the clinic. ("Step out of line and you'll lose your clinic.")

Now that the clique has been removed and a new patient-dominated board has been elected, HEW is pulling out an old favorite in its bag of counterinsurgency tricks: if you don't do what we say, we'll give the grant to someone else ("Step out of line and you'll lose your little empire"). In its October 3, 1979, grant award, HEW placed 20 conditions on the new board, in particular the requirement for immediate substantial cutbacks in services. If the new board fails to meet these anti-patient conditions, HEW will look for another organization to run the clinic (U.S. Department of HEW, 1979c). In that way, HEW is trying to repeat the cycle: trying to turn a new group of working class people into a new clique of poverty pimps, who take the side of HEW rather than of the patients whom they were elected to represent. Using the carrot (control over jobs and money) and the stick (do what we want or we'll give the grant to someone else), HEW will forever attempt to coopt and control the struggles of working class people for a voice in the decisions that affect their lives.

The Fight for True Patient Representation

The struggle for elections at MNHC was not a struggle to replace one set of poverty pimps with another. It was about democracy, about a voice for the majority of working class people in our country who have always been disenfranchised and ignored. The patients who won the recent MNHC election were chosen as representatives of the 800-member Patients Defense Association, and they pledged to represent the interests of the Association, of the patients of the health center, and not just of themselves.

In a statement made during the MNHC boycott, the Patients Defense Association spoke:

For too long, patient representation has been a sham at the health center. One set of so-called "community leaders" after another have gained control, claiming the support of the community that they did not have. Until now, patients have never organized for the principle of true patient representation. If patients are not organized, these small groups of "leaders" can continue to get in power and refuse to listen to us. We are trying to do something that we haven't seen done before: get patient representatives who are accountable to a democratic organization of hundreds of patients (Patients Defense Association, 1979).

Whether true patient representation can actually be achieved in the case of MNHC remains to be seen. The counterinsurgent pressure from HEW is strong and must be resisted every day. What counts is whether the new board will be able to consistently fight for the interests of the patients and against the control imposed by HEW.

—November 1979

REFERENCES

Braverman, Harry
    1974   Labor and Monopoly Capital. New York: Monthly Review Press.

Davis, Karen and Cathy Schoen
    1978   Health and the War on Poverty: A Ten Year Appraisal. Washington: The Brookings Institution.

Dixon, Marlene
    1978   "Abstract: The Degradation of Waged Labor and Class Formation on an International Scale." Synthesis, Vol. II, No. 3 (Spring): 50.

    1979   In Defense of the Working Class. San Francisco: Synthesis Publications.

Hartman, C. and Dan Feshbach
    1974   "Mission District Health Hustle." Common Sense (December).

Jonas, Susanne and Marlene Dixon
    1979   "Proletarianization and Class Alliances in the Americas." Synthesis, Vol. III, No. 1 (Fall): 1.

Martinez, Betita
    1979   "White, Black or Brown: A Poverty Pimp is a Poverty Pimp." Rebel Worker News Journal (June).

Patients Defense Association
1979 "The Fight for True Patient Representation."

Piven, Frances Fox and Richard A. Cloward
1971 Regulating the Poor: the Functions of Public Welfare. New York: Vintage Books.

Puga v. Hernandez
1979 Affidavits filed in the U.S. District Court, San Francisco, on September 7, 1979, by trustees, administrators and lawyers for MNHC.

Rebel Worker News Journal
1979 "Who Are Our Friends and Who Are Our Enemies? " (June).

U.S. Department of Health, Education, and Welfare
1979a Program Indicators.

1979b Memo from Region IX HEW office to San Francisco office of the FBI.

1979c October 3 Notice of Grant Award to MNHC.

Wright, Guy
1979a "A Sick Health Center." San Francisco Examiner (August 1).

1979b "Health Center Future." San Francisco Examiner (November 22).